Endorsements

Dr. Timothy Bagwell is in a category and a class all by himself. His prophetic acumen, passionate delivery, and personal character have catapulted the spiritual growth of The Potter's House of Dallas and all other ministries that have availed themselves of his expertise. I feel profoundly confident in advising all serious-minded Christians to saturate themselves with his wisdom. *The Prophetic Generation* is a clarion call from God as He uses Dr. Bagwell as His bugle.

Bishop T.D. Jakes Sr.
The Potter's House of Dallas, Inc.
CEO, TDJ Enterprises, LLP

An end-time prophet, pastor, and teacher, Tim Bagwell literally exemplifies the empowerment of the call of God on a believer's life. Knowing Tim Bagwell, his lovely wife, Gayla, and his sons, Adam and Aaron, and ministering in their church in Denver has made me realize that he is a great man with an anointed church. I love those dear saints. In so many ways they reflect Tim's anointed ministry, his scholarly insights into God's Word, and his passionate love and vision.

The late ORAL ROBERTS

I was excited to be asked to write an endorsement for Dr. Timothy Bagwell and his new book, *The Prophetic Generation*. The subject of the prophetic is something Dr. Bagwell is qualified to write about. He has demonstrated a lifetime of consistent participation in hearing from God and faithfully speaking what he has heard. Many in the Body of Christ believe in the prophetic but don't consistently participate in it. Sometimes the prophetic needs an advocate. Tim is that!

I could say a lot about the book, but let me instead say something about the author. I know Tim as a friend, the pastor of an outstanding megachurch, a dedicated husband to a beautiful wife, a successful father to two sons who have followed him in the ministry, and a proud grandfather. He's also a pretty good golfer! All of these things are important to know because a man who purports to prophetically "speak for God" needs to have both feet on the ground. I'm really excited to see the impact that this important work will have on the lives of many around the world. I believe you will feel informed and inspired by reading this book and—who knows?—maybe even develop a gift from God for hearing Him clearly and powerfully declaring what you hear! Thanks, Tim, for this powerful tool. I say read it and "speak"!

MIKE HAYES
Founder/Senior Pastor
Covenant Church, Dallas, TX

In this generation, the Lord has raised up strategic leaders equipped by the experience of time and testing and with a godly compassion to empower the Church to face the challenges of this fast-paced information age in which we live. Tim Bagwell is one of those rare individuals whose gifted spirit, transparent character, and integrity is a welcome breath of fresh air. I highly recommend his relevant and timely message to all those who desire truth. It lays down principles that are destined to impact your life and the world around you.

DR. MYLES MUNROE
Bahamas Faith Ministries

When I first heard the title, *The Prophetic Generation: Fearless and Uncompromising*, by my friend and colleague, Dr. Tim Bagwell, I was immediately intrigued. Any time our dear brother receives revelation, I am all ears. For Dr. Bagwell not only has a prophetic voice, he also has a prophetic mandate for transformation within the Body of Christ. He is a brooder with the Holy Ghost, and God speaks clearly and profoundly to him.

Furthermore, Pastor Tim also functions in the office of the prophet, something I have benefited from firsthand. In August of 2011, he was our special guest at Power and Praise Tabernacle in Flint, Texas. My father was still living at the time. I watched as this man, not given to much socializing nor fanfare, delivered for three consecutive nights, a powerful prophetic word to our house that not only helped to reset the course for Schambach Ministries, but it also expertly encouraged every minister in the house personally, and there were many present.

Since that time, the word spoken over my life has unfolded precisely as he delivered it. As my team experienced a powerful move of God in a tiny town in Peru, his words were ringing in the ears of several of my team members.

Perhaps my most memorable impression of Dr. Bagwell's visit with us was the day he came and sat to listen to my 85-year-old Papa, R.W. Schambach, deliver one of his last messages. I remember him kneeling before my elderly father, receiving the laying on of hands and a special impartation prayer.

Imagine my thoughts, when such a seasoned, effective servant of the Lord, would humble himself, and ask the Lord for more. That spoke volumes about a prophet, who lives what he preaches—a man committed to Holy Ghost, chain-destroying, prophetic revival—submitting himself to God's anointing in every way.

Let's go headlong into this great book, expecting God to speak to us words of encouragement and challenge, from one of His strongest prophetic voices and finest servants, Dr. Tim Bagwell.

DONNA J. SCHAMBACH
Pastor and Evangelist
Schambach Ministries International
www.schambach.org

THE PROPHETIC GENERATION

THE FEARLESS PROPHETIC AND UNCOMPROMISING GENERATION

DR. TIM BAGWELL

DESTINY IMAGE® PUBLISHERS, INC.

P.O. Box 310, Shippensburg, PA 17257-0310

"Promoting Inspired Lives."

This book and all other Destiny Image, Revival Press, MercyPlace, Fresh Bread, Destiny Image Fiction, and Treasure House books are available at Christian bookstores and distributors worldwide.

For a U.S. bookstore nearest you, call 1-800-722-6774.

For more information on foreign distributors, call 717-532-3040.

Reach us on the Internet: www.destinyimage.com.

ISBN 13 TP: 978-0-7684-0331-2

ISBN 13 Ebook: 978-0-7684-8569-1

For Worldwide Distribution, Printed in the U.S.A.

1 2 3 4 5 6 7 8 / 17 16 15 14 13

Dedication

I wish to dedicate this book to my wife
Gayla Jean Bagwell

You have stood with me through this incredibly challenging journey of ministry. Without your spirit of excellence, shepherd's heart, and creative mind, I would not have obtained the level of success in ministry that I have. Your love for God, family, and me have made my walk more productive and have helped me keep my priorities right.

I also wish to dedicate this book to my two sons
Adam and Aaron Bagwell

I believe you are two young eagles who will have a pivotal part in this prophetic generation. I am very proud of both of you and your passionate commitment to ministry. You are both uniquely gifted and will make your own distinctive impact for the kingdom of God.

Contents

FOREWORD

BY JOHN BEVERE

When the apostle Peter addressed the Jewish crowd on the Day of Pentecost, he spoke of a powerful generation of faith that would arise in the latter days. These men and women would shine the light of heaven into the darkness of a lost world. Armed with truth in the Spirit of God, they would champion Christ's cause on the earth. The book you now hold in your hands will empower you to take your place in this anointed generation.

My friend, Dr. Tim Bagwell, is a prophetic voice to this generation of believers. He walks in authority and power, and I believe his words hold immeasurable weight and value for every member of the Church. As you read *The Prophetic Generation*, you will grow in your revelation of God Himself: the God who draws near to us as we draw near to Him, and who reveals secrets to His friends (see James 4:8; Ps. 25:14).

I encourage you not only to read the words on these pages, but also to live them. As you lay hold of God's declarations over you, you will be positioned to walk into the destiny He intended for you.

The prophet Joel declared that all men and women under the new covenant would have the ability to speak prophetically (see Joel 2:28-29). You can, and must, learn to walk with authority, confidence, and accuracy in this expression of the Spirit. When you understand your place—and the place of our generation—in history, you will be stirred to fulfill the desires of God's heart for this time.

Friends, it is not enough for us only to know what God is saying. As those who have been given authority on this earth (see Ps. 115:16), we must speak His words so that His will can be done. In this hour, God is looking for righteous men and women who will boldly declare and move in what He proclaims. We must be unshaken by doubt or murmurs of dissension. We must be unwilling to draw back in fear. We must not allow the perversions or misinterpretations of the past to silence the prophetic voice in the present. We must be as God has foreseen: a victorious Church decisively destroying the devil's works.

For those who have questions about the office of the prophet or how to discern the trustworthiness of a prophetic word, Dr. Bagwell offers practical biblical insights. Through scriptural accounts of prophetic utterances, he will help you anticipate how God desires to move in your own life. I believe his testimony to the power of prophecy will generate a greater hunger in you for the *rhema* word of God.

This book is a valuable tool for all who desire to operate in the prophetic. Standing on the firm foundation of Jesus Christ, you will learn to hear God speak and to respond with vibrant faith. You will be encouraged to believe in what is unseen. And as you begin to speak in faith, you will be equipped to reach a lost world with the heart of the Father. Together, we can be the generation that readies the earth for Christ's return. Let us listen well and declare boldly—all for His glory.

John Bevere
Author and Speaker
Messenger International
Colorado Springs | United Kingdom | Australia

Foreword

by Mark Chironna

The Church is built on the foundation of the apostles and prophets, and Christ Jesus is the Chief Cornerstone. All too often in this twenty-first-century culture, the prophetic can be subject to one of two things: either it is dismissed altogether as irrelevant or those who have no accountability to apostolic oversight can misuse it. God intends the prophetic to have a significant expression in the Body of Christ and in the earth in order to bring about His eternal purpose in *"bringing many sons to glory"* (Heb. 2:10).

Over the years, I have had the privilege of connecting with some of the most significant, authentic, trustworthy, and seasoned prophetic voices in the kingdom of God on the earth. Among that number is one of the finest apostolic and prophetic voices I know of alive today, a dear friend, and someone who has paid the price to speak the word of the Lord into contexts involving large networks of leaders and in local churches around the globe.

Dr. Timothy Bagwell carries a signature anointing based on his calling in God that is distinctive, authoritative, transformative, and empowering! I have personally learned how to war a good warfare based on the things he has spoken into my life personally. I am so delighted that he has decided to put his heart into expressing the heart of God for this generation in this new book, *The Prophetic Generation*. It deserves a readership as wide as the move of God in the earth. Whatever place you occupy in the kingdom, this treatise will furnish you with insight, tools, and weapons to wage an effective, strategic, and tactical warfare against the forces of darkness as you pursue your God-designed and God-intended destiny.

We owe Dr. Bagwell a debt of gratitude for taking the time to instruct us in this mighty volume. May God multiply His truths in this book as He did the loaves and the fishes, and may the multitudes in this end-time move of the Spirit be richly fed.

MARK J. CHIRONNA, MA, PHD
Church On The Living Edge
Mark Chironna Ministries
Orlando, Florida

Introduction

A Prophetic Generation

So He humbled you, allowed you to hunger, and fed you with manna which you did not know nor did your fathers know, that He might make you know that man shall not live by bread alone; but man lives by every word that proceeds from the mouth of the Lord (Deuteronomy 8:3).

Moses's declaration from the 8th chapter of Deuteronomy is as clear-cut as the commandments God engraved on tablets of stone. The prophet understood God's ways and realized that physical sustenance is *never* enough. Although human beings might survive on bread, life is more than survival. Real life is released with every word that leaves God's lips.

After leading millions of slaves through barren wilderness for four decades, Moses knew it was time to remind them of this truth. The Israelites had "seen it all" on their journey—water gushing from stones, quail delivered by the wind, manna appearing like clockwork to satisfy their hunger—every day for 40 years. Yet, Moses knew their future success depended upon their ability to discern the deeper meaning of all they had experienced along the way.

The Israelites, whose lives and sustenance had been controlled by Pharaoh for 400 years, found themselves on their own—in the middle of nowhere! Yet, they saw every need satisfied. Not even so much as a shoe had worn out during their trek (see Deut. 29:5). In a desolate place where nothing grew and water was scant, divine provision had miraculously become a matter of course.

Despite the wonders they witnessed, they routinely forgot God's goodness. Miracles faded from the collective memory like flickers from a lightening bug. The Israelites' faith was up one day and down the next. They whined, murmured, and longed for the "amenities" of Egypt. Even after suffering through generations of brutality, captivity seemed a more viable option than the promise of dominion in the land of milk and honey.

Moses had been on the receiving end of the Israelites' short memories long enough to know they would need a refresher course before they set foot in the Promised Land. Not only were they fickle, but the generation that walked out of Egypt was dead and gone. The new generation had not known slavery. They were born into God's miraculous provision. They were accustomed to the cloud that shielded them by day and the pillar of fire that kept them by night. As far back as they could remember, manna was delivered daily, and always on time (see Exod. 13:21; 16:35).

Now things were about to change. The new generation would have to take the Promised Land and cultivate it. They would have to clear out their enemies and guard the territory they won. In order to *live* the promise, this generation of Israelites needed to understand the difference between mere bread and the absolute life that proceeds from God's mouth.

Moses knew what the difference was, and he was not about to take the revelation to the grave. His time was short and the pressures of conquest were coming. God's people needed what Moses had, so he shared it:

> When Moses reminded them that they did not live on bread alone he meant that even their food was decreed by the word of God. They had manna because it came by His command. It was therefore ultimately not bread that kept them alive but His Word! "Bread alone," that is, bread acquired independently of His Word, could not keep them alive.[1]

Unless they relied on God's proceeding word, the Israelites would exchange one form of bondage for another. Instead of being enslaved to Pharaoh, they would succumb to pride, deception, and human limitation. Moses knew this. He was a man whose priorities were clear: he would sooner have done without manna than exist without hearing from God.

The Savior whom Moses foreshadowed knew it too. After 40 days of fasting and temptation in the wilderness, Jesus was hungry and weary. Nevertheless, He stood on God's truth.

> *Now when the tempter came to Him, he said, "If You are the Son of God, command that these stones become bread."*
>
> *But* [Jesus] *answered and said, "It is written, '**Man shall not live by bread alone, but by every word that proceeds from the mouth of God**'"* (Matthew 4:3-4).

Always the opportunist, the devil offered Jesus a shortcut. A famished, natural-minded person might have found it attractive. But Jesus was not swayed. He knew His Father's faithfulness all too well to fall for the devil's devices. Jesus knew that bread could not generate life, but only maintain it.

Moses knew and Jesus knew. The Israelites heard, and now we must remember where life is found. Whether we are listening or allowing His words to fall on deaf ears, God is speaking. He is *always* speaking, and His words are all we need to live.

A Prophetic Birth

On the Day of Pentecost, the Church of Jesus Christ was born. It was a momentous day designed by God. Nothing about it fit into man's "box." Instead, the dramatic events set Jerusalem on edge and pushed hard against the religious thinking that had overtaken the place.

The meaning of Pentecost would force the overthrow of human notions. In an instant, routines and traditions were upended. The people were astounded and perplexed. They asked each other, *"Whatever could this mean?"* (Acts 2:12).

Struggling to manage the situation on their own terms, they tried to explain it away. Some mocked Jesus's disciples, saying, *"They are full of new wine"* (Acts 2:13). The mockers had a point. The disciples *were* full of new wine, but it was not the kind of wine some imagined it to be. This wine did not come from the grape, but from the True Vine (see John 15:1).

At the height of the tumult, Peter stood, bold as a lion and ready to set the record straight. No sooner had he begun to speak than he quoted the prophet Joel, who foretold the day when God would pour out His Spirit upon all people. Joel said that sons and daughters, both men and women, would prophesy. He said that young men would see visions and old men would dream dreams (see Joel 2:28-29; Acts 2:17-18).

Peter knew that day had come. Prophecy had been fulfilled before their eyes!

Today's Church

I wrote this book in part to say that the Church's prophetic story did not end on the Day of Pentecost or with the deaths of those who walked with Jesus. God has not pulled the prophetic plug. He never rescinded His plan. He set no expiration date on what He put in motion on the historic birth date of the Church.

The prophetic Church is in line with the working of God's eternal plan. Without exception, everything in His kingdom is released and activated through His spoken word. Scripture bears this out as far back as Creation, when the *"earth was without form, and void; and darkness was on the face of the deep"* (Gen. 1:2).

With a mighty *"God said"* (Gen. 1:3), the reversal of darkness and chaos began. Suddenly, there was light and a firmament. The waters were gathered and the earth brought forth vegetation. Lights in the heavens appeared and the seas were filled with life. Soon, birds soared overhead.

Then came the crowning of Creation: the making of man in God's image and likeness (see Gen. 1:26-27). God commanded man to *"be fruitful, and multiply"* and to *"have dominion"* (Gen. 1:28,26). God spoke His intention, and every word became physical reality.

That is exactly what God did when He birthed His Church. He released and activated a community of faith that would follow His example and act in His name.

By His design, the Church is a prophetic vehicle filled with believers who hear His proceeding word and speak it into the earth. This is not a passive Church, but a robust assembly of warriors determined to walk in the dominion established with a *God said* at Creation (see Gen. 1:28). In this hour, *we* are the warriors. We are the ones called to take back everything the devil has stolen. We are commissioned by God to pin Satan under our feet and keep him there.

Whether in seasons of resounding victory or drought, we are able in Him to war and win. I am convinced the day is coming when we will see tumors dissolved, blood diseases vanquished, financial difficulties reversed, and entire nations won for Christ—not once in a while, but every day, wherever we go.

That is the kind of Church God released and activated 2,000 years ago! It is not a Body guided by convenience or comfort, but a people who *"hunger and thirst for righteousness"*

(Matt. 5:6). The prophetic Church does not feed on skim milk, but on strong meat. Her people come early and stay late. They are not looking for user-friendly environments, but for churches that burn with the fire of God. They are willing to hit their knees and get their hands dirty. They don't mind when ministry gets messy; they long to destroy the works of the devil and are willing to look unusual in the world's eyes.

The prophetic Church is not for the rigidly religious, the face-saving, or the eternally immature. It is for those who will seek the kingdom at any cost.

> *"Blessed are those who hunger and thirst for righteousness, for they shall be filled"* (Matthew 5:6).

Why a Prophetic Generation?

A prophetic generation is more than a personal preference of mine. It is an end-time necessity. As John the Baptist did at Christ's advent, God's prophetic generation will prepare a dark and degraded world for the King's Second Coming.

Do you remember how John the Baptist described himself to the priests and Levites sent to question him? He responded by saying, *"I am 'the voice of one crying in the wilderness: make straight the way of the Lord'"* (John 1:23).

John prepared a generation for Messiah and connected centuries of prophecy to His advent. The Jews who recognized the Christ carefully examined His claims in light of prophecies that reached all the way back to Genesis 3:15.[2] Now, Messiah's appearing signaled a shift. For those willing to embrace it, a new dispensation was about to begin!

Prophetically speaking, John the Baptist lit the fuse. According to Luke 1:41, he bore witness to the Christ when he and Jesus were in their mothers' wombs! Jesus would later commend John, saying, *"Among those born of women there has not risen one greater than John the Baptist"* (Matt. 11:11).

John never pointed to himself, but always to the Christ. With prophetic clarity he said, *"I indeed baptize you with water; but One mightier than I is coming, whose sandal strap I am not worthy to loose. He will baptize you with the Holy Spirit and fire"* (Luke 3:16).

John was the strategic voice in Jesus's day. A new prophetic voice will precede the Second Coming of Christ. And I believe that voice was described in Joel's prophecy. It is not the sound of one man crying in the wilderness, but the voice of an entire generation—a prophetic generation that will declare His soon return and prepare the world for His arrival!

Foundation of the Prophetic Generation

In many quarters of today's Church, it is said that the prophetic and other gifts are not for today. They say the Church no longer needs prophets because God speaks to us through the Scriptures.

God most certainly speaks to us through the Scriptures, and powerfully so. However, first-century Jews had the Scriptures, including all of the prophetic books. Why then did God send John the Baptist? And why did Jesus endorse John's ministry? The Scriptures had already revealed the Messiah. Every Jew knew what Scripture said about Him. He stood in their midst, and *still* God sent His prophet to plow the road ahead of His Son.

Just as diligent Jews compared Christ's claims to Scripture, we must measure against Scripture every word passing over the pulpit or issuing from the seminary. If Scripture stated that the prophetic was for a season, I would believe it and be satisfied. However, Scripture says no such thing. Peter's first sermon from the 2nd chapter of Acts refers to and advocates the power of the prophetic. Nowhere did Peter add a disclaimer or expiry date.

And Peter was not alone. The apostle Paul also bore witness to the prophetic Church. He affirmed the prophetic gifts and the office of the prophet, which he declared to be one of five essential ministries established by God to equip and edify the Church. Consider his words:

> *And He Himself gave some to be* ***apostles, some prophets, some evangelists, and some pastors and teachers,*** *for the equipping of the saints for the work of ministry, for the edifying of the body of Christ, till we all come to the unity of the faith and of the knowledge of the Son of God, to a perfect man, to the measure of the stature of the fullness of Christ* (Ephesians 4:11-13).

Under the inspiration of the Holy Spirit, Paul ascribed enormous responsibility to all five offices, and particularly emphasized the foundational apostolic and prophetic offices:

> *Now, therefore, you are no longer strangers and foreigners, but fellow citizens with the saints and members of the household of God, having been*

> ***built on the foundation of the apostles and prophets,*** *Jesus Christ Himself being the chief cornerstone, in whom the whole building, being fitted together, grows into a holy temple in the Lord, in whom you also are being built together for a dwelling place of God in the Spirit* (Ephesians 2:19-22).

If God Himself gave (as Ephesians 4:11 declares) five distinct offices to serve the Body of Christ, and apostles and prophets are the foundation of God's household (as asserted in Ephesians 2:20), how can we justify the dismissal of any of them?

My point is not to craft an argument or stir controversy, but to sound a clarion call for fidelity to God's holy Word. He has given us multiple witnesses to the prophetic realm. The Scriptures not only reveal its existence, but also explain its purpose and application, as we will see in detail later.

Let me pose one more question for your prayerful consideration: Might we be the prophetic generation God has chosen to prepare the way for Christ's return? And, if we are that generation, will we embrace the call?

COMING TO TERMS

The New Testament offers three primary lists of spiritual gifts. The prophetic is mentioned in all three. Romans 12 and First Corinthians 12 refer to prophecy as one of the *charismata,* which are gifts distributed throughout the Body of Christ. Believers (ideally, *all believers,* according to Joel's prophecy) move in these gifts at the prompting of the Holy Spirit. Therefore, believers in all walks of life may prophesy.

There is a difference, however, between prophesying and being called as a prophet. Those called to the prophetic office named in Ephesians 4:11 bear a unique set of responsibilities, as we will see in future chapters.

My Hope for the Church

Our world is dark and growing darker as the return of Christ draws nearer. Each day, the anguish of our fallen world increases. Multiplied thousands breathe their last and are plunged into eternal darkness, while many of the living fall victim to demonic deceptions.

These dismal facts do not leave us hopeless. When Jesus preached His Sermon on the Mount, He saw our day coming. The Prophet and Savior, who is *"the same yesterday, today, and forever"* (Heb. 13:8), saw the Church age when He spoke these powerful words:

> *You are the salt of the earth; but if the salt loses its flavor, how shall it be seasoned? It is then good for nothing but to be thrown out and trampled underfoot by men. You are the light of the world. A city that is set on a hill cannot be hidden. Nor do they light a lamp and put it under a basket, but on a lampstand, and it gives light to all who are in the house. Let your light so shine before men, that they may see your good works and glorify your Father in heaven* (Matthew 5:13-16).

The Church of Jesus Christ will never be trampled underfoot. It is destined to glorify our Father in heaven. Yet, the

Church has an enemy, Satan, who desperately seeks to suppress the move of God's Holy Spirit in and through His people. It falls to us, therefore, to remember this truth: Satan is a defeated foe. He cannot keep the Church locked in complacency, timidity, political correctness, or any other device—unless we allow it.

The sooner we go "all in" with God, the sooner we defy the traditions of men and cling to His Word without reservation, the sooner we hunger for Him and His kingdom above all else, and the sooner His fresh anointing will flow from us to our world. The Holy Spirit stands ready to release an overflow—rivers of life to the hurting, the lost, and those whose lives hang by a thread.

Friend, I believe we are about to see the greatest harvest in all of history. Like the Israelites who saw wonders in the wilderness, we have seen too much to turn back now. The leeks, cucumbers, and garlic of Egypt cannot entice us back to captivity. Neither can the ease of manna draw us back into a barren land.

We are called to take the territory, cultivate it, and maintain dominion over it—all on the strength of God's proceeding word. Everything He has spoken is still at work, releasing and activating His will in the heavenlies and in the earth. His words are breaking yokes, removing burdens, opening the windows of heaven, and releasing the rain that reverses every demonic scheme.

God is speaking *right now* to His prophetic generation!

Notes

1. John F. Walvoord and Roy B. Zuck, editors, *Bible Knowledge Commentary* (Colorado Springs: Cook Communications

Ministries, 1983, 2000), CD-ROM, Biblesoft, Inc. (© 1994, 2003, 2006).

2. Genesis 3:15 says, *"And I will put enmity between you and the woman, and between your seed and her Seed; He shall bruise your head, and you shall bruise His heel."*

Chapter 1

Power of the Proceeding Word

In the beginning God created the heavens and the earth. The earth was without form, and void; and darkness was on the face of the deep. And the Spirit of God was hovering over the face of the waters. Then God said, "Let there be light"; and there was light (Genesis 1:1-3).

Physicists search the heavens and the earth for clues to the Creation. Weighty mathematical formulas attempt to explain all that happened in the formative moments of the universe. Thesis after thesis is proposed and argued, and still, science cannot wrap its collective mind around the power of a *God said.*

With words, God unleashed all that was needed to create and organize worlds. All of the energy and matter forming stars, planets, orbits, gravity, and space itself was released when

God spoke. His words are producing to this day: the universe continues to expand; planets continue in their orbits; stars continue to shine; the sun emits the light and heat needed to sustain life on earth.

It is easy to take this constancy for granted. Too easily, we focus inward and forget who is in charge. Our egocentric perspective intensifies when life goes upside down and loss is the only thing we see. Dogged by uncertainty, we pray for the rollercoaster ride to end. We search the horizon for the return of "normalcy" and ask, "Why, God? Why?" I've been there. There have been moments and even seasons when all I knew to do was to scratch my head and ask, "God, what's up with this?"

This is just an educated guess, but it's probably a good one: You have asked Him the very same question. Everyone has. For Christians, it is one of the ways we learn to listen for His voice. I have been around the adversity mountain enough times to know that God speaks in *every* circumstance. He uses our questions, and even our confusion and fears, to get our attention.

If we listen, we will hear Him reminding us, as He reminded the Israelites: *"Man shall not live by bread alone; but...by every word that proceeds from the mouth of the Lord"* (Deut. 8:3).

God is teaching us to hear Him. He is reminding us that everything we breathe, taste, touch, and see was created, not by a scientific formula or a random event, but with a *God said.* With His words, God reversed the darkness and filled the void described in Genesis 1:2. With each *God said,* chaos became order and emptiness became overflow. He opened His mouth and spoke into existence the remedy for every condition that was lacking or otherwise contrary to His plan.

God's antidote then and now is a *God said.* With one word from Him, disorder is set aright, demonic restraint becomes divine release, burdens are removed, and yokes are destroyed.

God Is a Speaking God

Everything in God's kingdom begins with Him speaking. He is a prophetic God who creates and reveals His plans, purposes, and will to His people. We are created in His image; therefore, every aspect of the prophetic Church begins in the character of our speaking God.

Speaking and thinking are, of course, connected. Yet I did not describe God as a thinking God. Clearly, God thinks. Isaiah spoke about His thoughts:

> *"For My thoughts are not your thoughts, nor are your ways My ways," says the Lord. "For as the heavens are higher than the earth, so are My ways higher than your ways, and My thoughts than your thoughts"* (Isaiah 55:8-9).

God is more than a thinking God. He is a speaking God. He did not complete the Creation on the strength of His thoughts. He chose to *speak* the worlds into being. As a changeless God, His creative methods have remained consistent. He used words to birth the Church on the Day of Pentecost. Specifically, they were the words He had spoken hundreds of years earlier through His prophet Joel:

> *I will pour out My Spirit on all flesh; your sons and your daughters shall prophesy, your old men shall dream dreams, your young men shall see visions. And also on My menservants and on My maidservants I will pour out My Spirit in those days* (Joel 2:28-29).

Before Peter began his powerful first sermon, he saw the connection between Joel's prophecy and the outpouring of the Holy Spirit. Joel's words did not merely attest to the events of Pentecost; his words had been released both to reveal and activate them.

God's words do more than record the minutes of a meeting. His words are life-containers. They are predictive, but they do more than foretell what is to come—they *create* what is to come. Whenever He speaks, some kind of genesis is released, as history demonstrates. By His speaking, worlds were created, the plan of salvation was established, the work of the cross was delineated (see Gen. 1; 3:15; Isa. 53).

When God speaks about your future, He is conveying more than a snapshot of the life ahead. By revealing it, He defines who you are and releases the provision needed to fulfill your identity. Every spiritual gift, every talent, and every opportunity involved with the completion of your destiny is set in motion when God speaks. Even the tools and methods needed to remove obstacles from your path are activated.

God's creative work does not happen in a vacuum. Even as God speaks to your future, the devil delivers dire predictions designed to repudiate Him. Demonic "prophecies" come in many forms: the abuse of a parent, a difficult diagnosis, an addiction, or a poor self-image. The enemy will use any "evidence" he can muster to convince you that you are not who God says you are. He will work continuously to persuade you that you are locked into your current circumstances.

Let me set the record straight where the devil and his stories are concerned. First of all, you *are* who God says you are. Secondly, no matter how dismal your situation looks, Satan's predictions are, by definition, lies! He *"does not stand in the truth, because there is no truth in him. When he speaks a lie, he speaks from his own resources, for he is a liar and the father of it"* (John 8:44).

If you come into agreement with the enemy's lies, you will diminish your destiny. But you are not called to live by his words; you are called to live by what God says. Satan's words are no match for God's!

NOT JUST THINKING, BUT SPEAKING

When circumstances go haywire, our minds want to think and re-think the problems. We dwell on what is wrong and we imagine what should be. Then we wait for something to change. But thinking is not enough. For darkness to give way to light and for chaos to become order, we must *speak*.

> *Whoever **says** to this mountain, "Be removed and be cast into the sea, and does not doubt in his heart, but believes that those things he says will be done, **he will have whatever he says"*** (Mark 11:23).

COMMUNICATION, GOD STYLE

God is a speaking God who continually communicates with His people. He is creative and able to reveal His plans, will, and purposes by unlimited means. He will approach you differently than He does me because His communication is perfectly tailored to be effective. As unique as each case is, some forms of prophetic expression (including those described below) are seen throughout Scripture.

Dreams

In Scripture, we see dreams impacting lives and even history. In the Book of Genesis, God spoke to Jacob's favorite son, Joseph, through two powerful dreams that crystallized Joseph's call and foretold his destiny. That destiny was fulfilled years later, when Joseph's rise to power in Egypt resulted in the saving of Israel:

> *Now Joseph had a dream, and he told it to his brothers..., "Please hear this dream which I have dreamed: There we were, binding sheaves in the field. Then behold, my sheaf arose and also stood upright; and indeed your sheaves stood all around and bowed down to my sheaf." ...Then he dreamed still another dream and told it to his brothers, and said, "Look, I have dreamed another dream. And this time, the sun, the moon, and the eleven stars bowed down to me"* (Genesis 37:5-7,9).

Visions

God often speaks through visions. He used one vision to convey to Peter His desire to save all people, not just Jews. The vision transformed Peter's perspective and set in motion his ministry to the Gentiles, which began in the household of Cornelius (see Acts 10:19-48):

> *Peter went up on the housetop to pray, about the sixth hour. Then he became very hungry and wanted to eat; but while they made ready, he fell into a trance and saw heaven opened and an object like a great sheet bound at the four corners, descending to him and let down to the earth. In it were all kinds of four-footed animals of the earth, wild beasts, creeping things, and birds of the air. And a voice came to him, "Rise, Peter; kill and eat"* (Acts 10:9-13).

The images God used helped Peter see that his outmoded religious ideas were limiting his effectiveness and obedience to God. He was called to minister to all kinds of people, wherever he found them, not just to the Jews.

Prophecy

Throughout the ages, God has spoken through prophecy. He Himself prophesied the Savior in Genesis 3:15. Soon after the Christ Child was born, God prepared Joseph and Mary for the difficult road ahead with a prophecy spoken through Simeon, a devout Jew who had eagerly awaited Messiah's birth:

> *Then Simeon blessed them, and said to Mary* [Jesus's] *mother, "Behold, this Child is destined for the fall and rising of many in Israel, and for a sign which will be spoken against (yes, a sword will pierce through your own soul also), that the thoughts of many hearts may be revealed* (Luke 2:34-35).

Angels

Scripture provides many examples of God speaking through angels. The well-known exchange between the archangel Gabriel and Mary revealed God's plan for the virgin's immaculate conception:

> *Now in the sixth month the angel Gabriel was sent by God...to a virgin betrothed to a man whose name was Joseph, of the house of David. The virgin's name was Mary. ...The angel said to her, "Rejoice, highly favored one, the Lord is with you; blessed are you among women!"* (Luke 1:26-28)

His Still Small Voice

God's speaking does not always involve intermediaries. This is especially true in the current dispensation. Yet, even in Old Testament times, God spoke directly to certain people. During a series of dramatic events, God revealed Himself to Elijah in a still small voice:

> *And behold, the Lord passed by, and a great and strong wind tore into the mountains and broke the rocks in pieces before the Lord, but the Lord was not in the wind; and after the wind an earthquake, but the Lord was not in the earthquake; and after the earthquake a fire, but the Lord was not in the fire; and after the fire a still small voice* (1 Kings 19:11-12).

These are just a few examples of how God communicates with us. The key is to understand that whenever and through whatever means He speaks, God is prophesying. In every case He is predicting, revealing, and creating what is to come.

God is speaking *to us.* He will use whatever means necessary to get our attention. I cannot tell you how He will speak to you individually. I know that when He does, His message will reverberate in your heart, and you will know that it is Him.

God Answers Our Chaos

Just as the *"earth was without form, and void; and darkness was on the face of the deep"* (Gen. 1:2), we experience personal seasons of disorder. One of Satan's most sinister tactics is to shame us by insinuating that our messes are unusual. The truth is that chaos, darkness, and emptiness have touched every life.

Before a man or woman is born again, life is continually dark, spiritually speaking. When the truth of the Gospel touches the heart, the lost soul receives the Savior and the spirit is instantly regenerated. From that moment on, light forces out the darkness. The emptiness caused by separation from God evaporates and divine order begins permeating the redeemed life.

The new birth results from a *God said.* His truth is spoken and, by His Spirit, faith is activated. Chaos is instantly rebuked and reversal begins. The sludge of sin is washed away and the fruit of righteousness becomes manifest. This is the spiritual genesis of a person being delivered *"from the power of darkness and conveyed...into the kingdom of the Son of His love"* (Col. 1:13).

With each subsequent *God said*—whether it comes through meditation on His Word or by any other means He uses—strongholds are progressively dismantled and demonic restraint is converted to divine overflow. Every form of oppression is pushed back so that the waters of life are set within proper boundaries and dry land appears (see Gen. 1:6-9).

Chaos, darkness, and emptiness are not God's will for us. He desires for us to abide in the light of His presence. His plan is for us to hear and embrace His life-filled words. He wants us to know that He is always speaking and that every word He says is designed to spark a new beginning.

Everything that exists began with a word from God. In his Gospel, John wrote:

> *In the beginning was the Word, and the Word was with God, and the Word was God. He was in the beginning with God. All things were made through Him, and without Him nothing was made that was made* (John 1:1-3).

John was referring specifically to Jesus, *the* Word of God, being present and active in the Creation. Yet, John's inspired words have implications for our lives today.

In every beginning, there is a word. Nothing begins without God speaking. Your genesis was and is in your *God said.* It did not begin at your physical birth; God's proceeding word predated your birth. He had you and your divine destiny in mind before you were conceived. Then at some point, when you acknowledged your *God said* and took it to heart, the spiritual genesis already released began to manifest in the natural world.

Consider Peter. He was born long before Jesus approached him on the shores of Galilee. Peter's genesis as the great apostle from Scripture began in the mind of God before Peter was even conceived. It was activated in Peter's heart when Jesus told him and his brother Andrew: *"Follow Me and I will make you become fishers of men"* (Mark 1:17).

From that point forward, Peter was on a destiny path that he had not previously considered. Yet, that was not the end of Peter's chaos. Three years later, he misrepresented his Master's intent and sliced off a man's ear. Even worse, he denied that he even knew Jesus three times. After His resurrection, however, Jesus restored Peter. Even so, Peter would eventually be accused of hypocrisy and rebuked by Paul for "Judaizing" the Gospel (see Gal. 2:11-16).

Despite his failings, Peter's *God saids* continued working in his life. The fiery apostle fulfilled his mission and left the earth a man transformed by the proceeding word of God! This happened because Peter allowed Jesus to speak to his darkness.

Why not follow Peter's example? When darkness rises up against your life, let God speak to it. Let your response to adversity be a "Thus saith the Lord." Use your prophetic voice to reissue your *God said*, and He will reverse the darkness.

The Rhema Sword

The value of words cannot be overestimated; therefore, it is discussed throughout Scripture. In his letter to the Ephesians, Paul described the components of the believer's spiritual armor. All but one of the pieces are defensive; they serve to protect against demonic attack. Only one is an offensive weapon: *"the **sword of the Spirit,** which is the word of God"* (Eph. 6:17).

In physical battle, a sword can do tremendous harm. One good slash can put your enemy out of commission and end his onslaught against you. The spiritual sword, the Word of God, is far more powerful than any earthly or demonic weapon could be. God's Word is the ultimate weapon of spiritual warfare.

Ephesians 6:17 specifically refers to the *rhema* word of God. One definition of the Greek word *rhema* is "that which is or has been uttered by the living voice."[1] In other words, a rhema word is your *God said.* It is more than a word from the Bible (*i.e.,* the *logos,* or written Word of God). A rhema word is a spiritual activator.

Rhema is what caused Peter to obey Jesus when He said, *"Follow Me"* (Mark 1:17). When you receive a rhema word, it speaks directly and specifically to *you.* It sheds fresh light in your heart and on your situation. It reveals and explains something that is essential to the divine unfolding of your life.

The activation of a rhema word issues sovereignly from the throne of God. It will shake you from the crown of your head to the soles of your feet. It will ignite a fire in your belly. It might cause you to shake or weep or even to fall to the floor. A rhema word might start you dancing, shouting, or clapping your hands. In short, a rhema word will rattle your cage!

Every Christian is called to build his or her life upon the written Word of God. But your *God said*—your rhema word—is custom-fitted for you alone. It is an intimate word that fits like a glove and causes you to perceive something that others cannot. It will inspire and carry you through difficulties. It will cause you to persevere to the end, knowing that God is faithful, no matter the odds against you.

You can receive a rhema word while reading your Bible. Rhema can also be delivered through the words of a prophet, or in a dream or through a vision. Rhema can even enter your heart through the still small voice that Elijah heard on the mountain.

A rhema word is your sword, your "Thus saith the Lord," with which to slash the devil, silence his voice, and overcome his demonic attacks. When you have a rhema word, you can stand on it and proclaim: "I don't care what the devil throws at me. The Word of God sustains my life. Everything God has said or will ever say is already settled in heaven!" (See Psalm 119:89).

Humility and Hunger

God spoke to Israel in many ways. Of course, He spoke through Moses. But He also spoke through the movements of the cloud which told the people when to camp and when to move on. Perhaps most riveting was the sound of His voice on Mount Sinai (see Deut. 8:3; Exod. 40:36-37; 19:19).

God was a speaking God then, and He is a speaking God now.

I have never had a cloud lead me from one place to another, nor have I heard God's physical voice reverberate atop the Rocky Mountains. Yet, I know God speaks now every bit as much as He did in Moses's day. It is His nature to speak—and we desperately need to hear from Him.

You probably haven't spent 40 years crisscrossing the desert in the same old pair of shoes, but if you are anything like me, you have had a wilderness experience or two. Thankfully, God is never silent through our wanderings. He converts each step into a teachable moment, *if we will but listen.* His ongoing instruction protects us now and prepares us for tomorrow's journey.

God's lessons always involve two necessary spiritual conditions: our humility and hunger. Remember what Moses told Israel about God's "teaching methods" in the wilderness:

> *So He humbled you, allowed you to hunger, and fed you with manna which you did not know nor did your fathers know, that He might make you know that man shall not live by bread alone; but man lives by every word that proceeds from the mouth of the Lord* (Deuteronomy 8:3).

After more than 400 years of enslavement, Israel had a lot to learn. They were not called to remain in slavery; they were slated to conquer Canaan. This demanding role could not be mastered without God. Therefore, He positioned the Israelites to hunger, not so much for food, but for Him.

Their dependence upon Him was crucial, yet they resisted it. They probably felt vulnerable, as we often do. But God's plan was not meant to harm them; He would not lead His people into the desert to starve them. His methods were designed to erase their dependence upon idols, slave masters, and human strength.

God kept them hungry enough not to walk away. He knew that if they went forward without Him, they would perish. So He spoke to them about their ungodly dependencies and used hunger to develop the humility they needed to succeed. Until they learned that He was all they needed, they would continue wandering.

God speaks in our deserts too. He points to our promised land and calls us to conquer. He pulls down our idols—money, fame, pride, and pleasures—by revealing their hollowness and unreliability. In His love, He positions us to rely on Him alone.

If we are listening, we realize that our careers cannot satisfy us; neither can big houses and the right cars. Nothing we can devise can quench our deepest longings. His speaking addresses our hunger. It encourages and positions us to let go of the past and move forward with Him.

If you intend to stay on course with God, you might as well know that hunger is part of the package. It is not a curse, but a blessing. The hunger He allows will keep your eyes trained on Him and your ears listening intently for His proceeding word.

Bread Versus Manna

What was the purpose of the Israelites' wilderness experience? Why did God feed them with manna? Clearly, God is mighty and able to provide by whatever means He chooses. Therefore, we have to conclude that His decision to rain down manna involved more than earthly convenience and a supernatural supply chain. The heavenly delivery of manna was designed to *say something.*

The message of God's manna was tied to its unique properties. We tend to think of bread and manna as being alike. Nutritionally speaking, they served the same purpose; but they are not the same. Manna filled the Israelites' bellies much as bread would have done, but bread was a familiar food source. All bread—Italian bread, Wonderbread, flatbread, or even pizza crust—is made from grain, which comes from seed. The Israelites knew all about seed; they knew about sowing, watering, and harvesting it. Until God sent it, they knew nothing about manna.

Manna didn't come from a seed; it came directly from God. Apart from His speaking, manna could not have appeared. There was no way for the Israelites to sow it, harvest it, or replicate it. They could not even imagine it! Manna was the product of God's speaking into a specific situation with a definite purpose for a particular group of people at a particular time.

The details of manna creation point to the crux of Moses's message: *"Man shall not live by bread alone; but man lives by every word that proceeds from the mouth of the Lord"* (Deut. 8:3). When the Israelites ate manna, they were not living by way of bread, but by that which proceeded directly from the mouth of God! He spoke manna into existence and sent the exact amount needed: a day's worth for five days a week, and two days' worth on the sixth day. *The Israelites literally lived on God's proceeding word!*

Manna touched the Israelites' lives on every level and taught them several key lessons:

- It demonstrated God's commitment to their well-being.
- It confirmed His ability to provide in extreme circumstances.
- It revealed the reliability of His promises.
- It exposed their utter dependence on Him.
- It substantiated the creative power that is released every time He speaks.

These messages permeated the Israelites' wilderness experience. God repeated them by many other means, including the pillar of fire that guided them by night, the cloud that shielded them from the blistering sun by day, and the water that gushed from rocks. These were purely supernatural occurrences. They could not be explained apart from God's involvement. All of them were critical and seemingly impossible forms of provision; and all of them were revealed and created by God's speaking.

Many of us are so familiar with the Exodus accounts that we have become desensitized to them. We say, "Oh, yes, I know that," and move on. Without realizing it, we miss the exquisiteness of God's dealings by reducing them to the level of mythology or legend. But I am here to tell you that these truths were recorded in Scripture for a reason—to realign us with God's prophetic reality.

These "stories" reveal the power and potential inherent in God's proceeding word. Understanding His purpose in sending manna can deliver you out of your wilderness experiences. The reason is simple: as long as you believe you can sustain yourself on something you can find or do or plant, God will allow you to try. You might be within one step of possessing your promised land, but until you realize where your life is found, you will not step foot outside the wilderness.

Nowhere to Run

Have you ever shied away from reliance on God? Have you ever fled His call? Many well-known "Bible characters" did. Jonah was one. He heard God's call to Nineveh and headed for Tarshish instead.

Jonah chose his own way. He tried to ignore God's proceeding word. The results were disastrous. Instead of escaping his assignment, Jonah took the grand tour of a whale's belly. He was steeped in digestive juices for three nights until the giant creature vomited him out.

This was not the mode of transportation Jonah had envisioned for his escape. From God's perspective, the accommodations were less important than Jonah's getting the message—and he *did* get the message. Draped in layers of seaweed and a host of unmentionable substances, a humbled Jonah went to Nineveh. He understood that even if he ignored his *God said,* he could never escape it.

You cannot escape your *God said* either. You can document your disbelief on your iPad and share it on your blog, but He will keep on speaking. You can bawl and squall and decry the inconvenience of it all. You can even plead your own incompetence, but your rhema word will echo all the way to Tarshish. You will never shake off the word God speaks to you.

Why would you want to? God's proceeding word is the ultimate provision. Whatever your circumstances, His proceeding word answers every need and every question. Paul understood this perfectly. He had experienced great abundance and great deprivation. Yet he would not quit. He said, *"I know how to be abased, and I know how to abound. Everywhere and in all things I have learned both to be full and to be hungry, both to abound and to suffer need"* (Phil. 4:12).

Paul knew that his circumstances were not the issue. They defined neither him nor his destiny. Paul's life was sustained by truth. He fed, not on bread alone, but on every word that proceeded from the mouth of God. As a result, he was able to say, *"I have fought the good fight, I have finished the race, I have kept the faith"* (2 Tim. 4:7).

Your Life Connection

The connection to God's life is not found in gifts, talents, abilities, relationships, or access to high places. Although God can use our aptitudes and other accoutrements to bring His purposes to pass, they do not yield the life found in a single *God said.*

God's proceeding word is the umbilical cord that delivers *zoe* life to all aspects of your being. It kindles His plan in your heart and sets you on a destiny course that you could have never imagined. Your *God said* will impregnate you with His love for people, nations, and His kingdom purposes!

When your life connection is in place, your sense of purpose will not quit. When down is up and in is out, you will prevail and accomplish your God-ordained mission. You will incline your ear for His proceeding word because you know He is a speaking God.

> *"Your ears shall hear a word behind you, saying, 'This is the way, walk in it,' whenever you turn to the right hand or whenever you turn to the left"* (Isaiah 30:21).

Think on This

Is there a *God said* burning in your heart? What kind of life is it bringing forth? How has it changed you? If your *God said* is sitting "on the shelf," how did it get there? Did God tell you to shelve it? Why or why not?

Note

1. *Blue Letter Bible,* Dictionary and Word Search for *"rhema"* (Strong's 4487), Blue Letter Bible, 1996–2011, http://www.blueletterbible.org/lang/lexicon/lexicon.cfm?Strongs=G4487&t=KJV (accessed November 17, 2011).

Chapter 2

Birth of the Prophetic Church

But Peter, standing up with the eleven, lifted up his voice, and said unto them, Ye men of Judaea, and all ye that dwell at Jerusalem, be this known unto you, and hearken to my words: for these are not drunken, as ye suppose, seeing it is but the third hour of the day. But this is that which was spoken by the prophet Joel... (Acts 2:14-16 KJV).

It was a feast day for the Jews and Jerusalem was hopping. As was their annual custom, the faithful had gathered from many nations to commemorate the giving of the Law at Mount Sinai. Although the feast was marked by centuries of tradition, the celebration would be anything but conventional.

Each year, the waving of the sheaf of firstfruits occurred 50 days before Pentecost. This year, by divine clockwork, *the* firstfruits arose from the dead 50 days before the same sacred feast. (See First Corinthians 15:20-23.) As Luke explained under the inspiration of the Holy Spirit, Pentecost had *"fully come"* (Acts 2:1 KJV). The Church was about to be born.

After 40 days in the presence of the resurrected Jesus, the disciples then spent ten days waiting in the upper room. They were doing exactly what Jesus told them to do when He said: *"Behold, I send* ***the Promise of My Father*** *upon you; but tarry in the city of Jerusalem until you are endued with power from on high"* (Luke 24:49).

The Promise was the Holy Spirit. After the disciples tarried, the Holy Spirit came, just as Jesus said He would. His arrival upset the status quo and transformed the 120. Speaking in languages not their own, they spilled out of the upper room and caused a citywide commotion. The Bible tells the story best:

> *When the day of Pentecost was fully come, they were all with one accord in one place. And suddenly there came a sound from heaven as of a rushing mighty wind, and it filled all the house where they were sitting. And there appeared unto them cloven tongues like as of fire, and it sat upon each of them. And they were all filled with the Holy Ghost, and began to speak with other tongues, as the Spirit gave them utterance. And there were dwelling at Jerusalem Jews, devout men, out of every nation under heaven. Now when this was noised abroad, the multitude came together, and were confounded, because that every man heard them speak in his own language. And they were all amazed and marvelled, saying one to another, Behold, are not*

> *all these which speak Galilaeans? And how hear we every man in our own tongue, wherein we were born? Parthians, and Medes, and Elamites, and the dwellers in Mesopotamia, and in Judaea, and Cappadocia, in Pontus, and Asia, Phrygia, and Pamphylia, in Egypt, and in the parts of Libya about Cyrene, and strangers of Rome, Jews and proselytes, Cretes and Arabians, we do hear them speak in our tongues the wonderful works of God. And they were all amazed, and were in doubt, saying one to another, What meaneth this?* (Acts 2:1-12 KJV)

Can you imagine the scene? The amazement? The sound? Peter and his fellow disciples had experienced something inexplicable and entirely new to humankind—something they would not and could not keep to themselves. The evidence of a shift was too explosive to conceal: the disciples spoke fluently in languages they did not know. Those who had gathered in Jerusalem recognized those languages as their own. The phenomenon boggled their minds. Reeling, people asked, *"What meaneth this?"*

"This Is That"

"Others mocking said, These men are full of new wine" (Acts 2:13 KJV). The sights and sounds on the Day of Pentecost drove the Jews to their wits' end. There *had* to be an explanation for the disciples' bizarre behavior, and drunkenness seemed as good a rationale as any. Peter, however, knew better, and said so:

> *Peter, standing up with the eleven, lifted up his voice, and said unto them, Ye men of Judaea, and all ye that dwell at Jerusalem, be this known unto you, and hearken to my words:* ***For these are not drunken, as ye suppose,*** *seeing it is but the third hour of the day.* ***But this is that which was spoken by the prophet Joel;*** *and it shall come to pass in the last days, saith God, I will pour out of My Spirit upon all flesh: and your sons and your daughters shall prophesy, and your young men shall see visions, and your old men shall dream dreams: and on My servants and on My handmaidens I will pour out in those days of My Spirit; and they shall prophesy* (Acts 2:14-18 KJV).

Peter was lucid and perceived exactly what was going on. Immediately, he recognized the connection between the day's events and what Joel had prophesied hundreds of years earlier. He did not begin his sermon with the prophet's ancient words, however. Instead, he began by addressing the accusations of drunkenness. Notice that Peter did not outright refute the scoffers' claims. He said, "*These are not drunken,* ***as ye suppose***" (Acts 2:15 KJV).

What a provocative answer! The Bible does not record the reactions to this part of Peter's sermon, but I can imagine people in the crowd asking, "Well, are these people drunk or aren't they?"

Peter knew that he and the other 119 were under the influence, but not that of alcohol. They were under the divine influence of the promised Holy Spirit. The accusations of inebriation were designed to make people suspicious of the day's events. But Peter understood the magnitude of what was happening. The very foundation stones of Judaism and human thought were being shaken. Therefore, Peter chose his words with precision. Like a prophetic sharpshooter, he aimed them, and fired.

In the opening salvo of the first sermon on the first day of the Church of Jesus Christ, Peter unapologetically declared the prophetic nature of the upheaval being witnessed in Jerusalem. Of all the things he might have chosen to say, and of all the things that might have seemed pertinent or wise, Peter made this succinct and unceremonious statement: "This isn't what you think. *This is that* which Joel prophesied" (see Acts 2:15-16).

Peter sliced through the confusion and deception whirling around him and fixed the people's focus on the proceeding word of God. By revelation of the Holy Spirit, Peter pointed back in time to the forward-looking, future-creating words spoken by a revered prophet. In the Church's very first sermon on her inaugural day, Peter cleared the air of distractions and presented the crux of God's eternal purpose for the fullness of Pentecost. He did it by simply declaring the scriptural foundation of God's prophetic Church.

Peter's "this is that" identified a move of God that had already been activated: the formation of an army of prophetic men and women of all ages. Although this army first assembled on the Day of Pentecost, their march would continue through coming centuries. It would be fueled by prophetic utterances of all kinds that would reach even to the end-time prophetic generation and the great revival that would usher in the Lord's return.

The comprehensive aspects of this move—the idea of young, old, rich, poor, male, and female being released into the fullness of the prophetic—was a shot across the bow of Satan's kingdom. The enemy's worst fears were being realized. Jesus had been crucified; but legions of prophetic voices were raised to speak in His name!

The Church Joel and Peter prophesied of is a powerful Church. Wherever and whenever its prophetic anointing is released, it crushes the dark works of Satan and his minions. No wonder his attack against the prophetic has been so broad, so enduring, and so fierce.

THE LAW OF FIRST MENTION

Firsts are important. The idea of "first" was stressed to the extreme on the Day of Pentecost. By God's design, the very first words in the first sermon preached on the first day of the Church of Jesus Christ established a spiritual framework that affects us to this day. Likewise, the first mention of topics in Scripture is important in establishing the topic's overall context.

> The first time any subject is introduced in the Bible is of special significance. The Holy Spirit gives the clue there to the place and significance of that subject as it relates to the whole Bible. We can see at the time of its first mention how a matter is viewed by God Himself.[1]

Peter's quoting of Joel's prophecy was not a first mention in Scripture. It was, however, the first time the connection had been drawn between the prophet's words and the real-time events that unfolded on the Day of Pentecost.

Prophetic Shift

Peter quoted only an excerpt from the 2nd chapter of the Book of Joel. The book's overall theme is weighty—the broad point being the coming of the day of the Lord. Joel began his book with a warning and description of God's judgment, and a fervent call to repentance.

Peter did not focus on Joel's dark predictions. He selected only the passage that spoke of the outpouring of the Spirit. Under the unction of the Holy Spirit, Peter spoke only that which would release what God planned for that day.

Peter's sermon covered a lot of territory. Not only did it proclaim the birth of the prophetic Church, but it also reflected the dispensational shift that had just occurred. Remember that Jesus's sermons were preached prior to His sacrifice, resurrection, and ascension, during the dispensation of the Law. Until His blood was shed and He rose again and ascended to the right hand of the Father, the Law would remain in place to tutor God's people (see Gal. 3:24).

Now, the cross was a finished work, the Church age had begun, and Jesus's promise of the Holy Spirit had been fulfilled. The reasons for Jesus's instructions to tarry were no longer in question (see Luke 24:49). Prior to the outpouring of the Holy Spirit, the disciples would have been ill equipped—their message to the world would have been incomplete. When God's prophetic vehicle was finally prepared to launch, the disciples left the upper room, entered the public arena, and preached the Gospel.

The Day of Pentecost changed everything. The disciples were filled with the Holy Spirit and the fire of God. Their boldness would soon change the world. Confusion about

Christ's crucifixion was dispelled and His glory was manifested in Jerusalem's streets. People spoke in other tongues, bearing witness to what God was doing and would continue to do throughout the Church age. And 2,000 years later, we are part of what they testified to that day!

Three-Point Strategy

"This is that" spoke volumes to Peter's listeners. His point was that God Himself had revealed His plan centuries earlier. Now, its reality was unfolding, without discrimination. It was designed to transform people in all demographic groups. Its fulfillment was intended to be seen in the life of every Christ follower. This was the kind of Church God called into being: a Church immersed in the rich anointing and influence of the Holy Spirit.

The reality of the supernatural could not be denied. Nor could the passage Peter quoted on the Day of Pentecost be clearer or more dramatic:

> *And it shall come to pass afterward that I will pour out My Spirit on all flesh; your sons and your daughters shall prophesy, your old men shall dream dreams, your young men shall see visions. And also on My menservants and on My maidservants I will pour out My Spirit in those days* (Joel 2:28-29).

Jews were familiar with Joel's prophecy, but now, they were living it. Because it was no longer for *someday,* they had to come to terms with it. In an instant, the status quo was changed by three strategic components of the prophecy:

1. Both sons and daughters will prophesy. The Holy Spirit does not select or deselect vessels on the basis of gender. Men and women are called by God to move in the power of His Holy Spirit.

2. Old men and young men will experience the prophetic. The term *old men* speaks not of a specific age range but of those who are mature. There is no age discrimination where the move and power of the Holy Spirit are concerned.

3. The terms *menservants* and *maidservants* refer to people of low status, including slaves. By God's own decree, social status would not exclude anyone from the infilling of the Holy Spirit and His prophetic anointing.

The prophetic Church is a diverse and vibrant Body. It was birthed by God to achieve His aim—to reach the four corners of the world with the Gospel of Jesus Christ.

God's Prophetic "Vehicle"

It's important to remember that whenever God speaks, He is prophesying—but His words are more than predictive. His words *create* what He speaks. The words that leave God's mouth always generate something that did not exist before He spoke. On the Day of Pentecost, God's prophetic vehicle in the earth was released to its mission.

It is amazing to realize that God actually speaks to and through imperfect people. The power and majesty of His speaking stand in stark contrast to the corruption and depravity of our world. Yet, God does not reserve His words for those who are perfect (if perfection were even possible). Nor did He reserve His Son—the Living Word—for the "perfect" season. Jesus walked in the midst of a generation as unseemly as any other. He called His contemporaries a *"generation of vipers"* (Matt. 12:34 KJV), *"an evil and adulterous generation"* (Matt. 12:39), *"a wicked and adulterous generation"* (Matt. 16:4), a *"faithless and perverse generation"* (Matt. 17:17), and *"a sinful generation"* (Mark 8:38).

Do those descriptions ring a bell? Yes! They describe *our* generation. Since the Fall of Man, the world has been steeped in sin. If sin were to limit God's love, the world would have been doomed almost from the start. Instead, God's proceeding word is His remedy for darkness.

Right in the thick of the perversity of their day, Peter and his accomplices proclaimed the birth of God's prophetic vehicle. It stood as a new beginning—a genesis from the mouth of God. It was a preordained, God-activated move like nothing humans had ever seen. Peter described a new generation of men, women, boys, girls, old, young, free, and oppressed people who were called to operate in God's prophetic power. Their world was dark, decaying, and desecrated, but every *God said* would reverse the disintegration. God's new prophetic vehicle would be His public address system in the earth. The world's communication systems have become increasingly poisonous since the first century. Division, hatred, slander, and deception are the trademarks of earthly discourse. But even today, God has the antitoxin for our poisons: it is a *God said* in the mouth of His people.

God established His Church to be salt and light. He knew the world would grow darker and darker before His Second Coming, but His people were to hold their ground. Through the apostle Paul, He instructed His prophetic Church to conduct themselves in ways that defied the world's perversity:

> *Do all things without complaining and disputing, that you may become blameless and harmless, children of God without fault in the midst of a crooked and perverse generation, among whom you shine as lights in the world, holding fast the word of life, so that I may rejoice in the day of Christ that I have not run in vain or labored in vain* (Philippians 2:14-16).

God told the Philippians to declare the light to a warped generation. And He is telling us the same thing. We are His prophetic vehicle created to drive away darkness and bring His remedy to a sick and dying world. Yes, we live in an evil generation, but God never meant for us to leave it the way we found it. It is His plan for us to proclaim the light and reverse the darkness.

Identity of the Prophetic Church

The Church was birthed to bear the nature of God. When He speaks, something is activated. When we speak in His name, we activate the things He desires.

This is the core message of Peter's "this is that" statement. Peter's sermon, especially the excerpt from Joel 2:28-29, stamped upon the Church's birth certificate its prophetic character and function. Just as the feast of Pentecost was celebrated in honor of the giving of the Law, the full coming of Pentecost proclaimed an age in which every human would speak God's heart in prophetic power.

The message of the Day of Pentecost was aligned with Moses's appreciation of God's heart for the prophetic. Centuries earlier, when men began prophesying in the camp, Joshua saw it as an affront to Moses's leadership. Moses saw it differently, however. His perspective sheds light on the divine identity of the Church:

> *But two men had remained in the camp: the name of one was Eldad, and the name of the other Medad. And the Spirit rested upon them. Now they were among those listed, but who had not gone out to the tabernacle; yet they prophesied in the camp. And a young man ran and told Moses, and said, "Eldad and Medad are prophesying in the camp."*
>
> *So Joshua the son of Nun, Moses' assistant, one of his choice men, answered and said, "Moses my lord, forbid them!"*
>
> *Then Moses said to him, "Are you zealous for my sake? Oh, that all the Lord's people were prophets and that the Lord would put His Spirit upon them!"* (Numbers 11:26-29)

God's prophetic Church is nondiscriminatory—all are called to move in the prophetic (according to the level of their faith, as we will see later). For the record, I am not endorsing a prophetic free-for-all. Foolishness is not what Joel and Moses were talking about. There is a difference between promoting prophetic silliness and helping believers walk in the fullness of their giftings. The prophetic must be protected with wisdom. The Church must be aware of the price and integrity the prophetic demands. Nevertheless, it must never be hoarded or restricted to "certain" people.

Joel 2:28-29 describes the identity of the Church. Peter's "this is that" reminds us that we must re-identify with our prophetic nature. To maintain this identity will require perseverance and the refusal to accept a diluted version of the Gospel and the Church. As I said in the Introduction, we must maintain our fidelity to God's Word.

For example, Ephesians 4:11-12 lists five offices in the Body of Christ: apostle, prophet, evangelist, pastor, and teacher. Where did we get the idea that we were appointed to cherry-pick those offices? When did God say that apostles and prophets were no longer needed? If pastors are still needed, so are the other offices. God designed them to complement one another in meeting the broad range of needs He knew would arise in His Church.

We are OK with teachers, especially in Sunday school. Most every denomination is comfortable with that. In some quarters, we are pickier about evangelists. We give them our stamp of approval if they fit a certain mold. Most of us are comfortable with Billy Graham (as we should be). But not every evangelist is called to be like Billy Graham.

My point is that the Word of God is the final authority, not the whims of men. The prophetic is mentioned in all gift listings (see Eph. 4; Rom. 12; 1 Cor. 12). It is listed as one of the five ministry offices, and it was referred to in Scripture *after* the birth of the Church. For example, when Paul sought to encourage Timothy's faith and ministry, he referred to the continued importance of the prophetic, saying, *"This charge I commit to you, son Timothy,* ***according to the prophecies previously made concerning you,*** *that by them you may wage the good warfare"* (1 Tim. 1:18).

Why would Paul make such a statement if prophecy were not for the Church? And if it were only for the first-century Church, why doesn't Scripture say so?

We must have integrity in this. We cannot cling to doctrines simply because they are taught from the pulpit. We must be like the Bereans who listened to the teaching of Paul and Silas, and *"...received the word with all readiness, and searched the Scriptures daily to find out whether these things were so"* (Acts 17:11). We must know what the Bible says. The very identity of the Church is at stake.

Point of Resistance

Resistance to the prophetic is a demonically inspired condition. It is often masked by subtlety and what resisters call "wisdom." In churches worldwide, leaders shut down even talk of the prophetic by saying, "People can't understand such things."

Really? If that were a valid argument, then it is high time we quit preaching salvation and the blood of Christ. We say, "Jesus has saved me and cleansed me with His blood." We know these things are true because the Holy Spirit bears witness with our spirits that they are (see Rom. 8:16). But can you really wrap your natural mind around the idea that a Man died on a cross, shed His blood, and relieved you for all eternity from the guilt of past, present, and future sin?

What about the Trinity? Has your natural mind figured out how that works? Mine hasn't, but I still believe it and preach it without apology. Paul said, *"The carnal mind is enmity against God; for it is not subject to the law of God, nor indeed can be"* (Rom. 8:7). He also said, *"We walk by faith, not by sight"* (2 Cor. 5:7). The natural mind cannot fully grasp any of these concepts. It is by faith and the revelation of the Holy Spirit that we embrace them.

"We walk by faith, not by sight" (2 Corinthians 5:7).

The human desire to reduce spiritual things to carnal formulas is the very reason the New Age movement is so popular. New Age teachings (from Zen Buddhism to Hinduism to Transcendental Meditation and more) appeal to the carnal mind. They are works-based and therefore comfortably "logical."

So, should we begin marketing these easily packaged concepts and quit preaching the finished work of the cross? Most Christian leaders would say, "No! Of course not!" and I would agree with them. Nevertheless, I am confident that some would vehemently oppose my stand regarding the scriptural operation of the prophetic gifts.

The only argument I will make is that of the full Gospel. It is not up to leaders to decide what people can or cannot believe. It is up to leaders to present the truth and let the people decide how they will respond to it. Any Christian leader who backs away from the Gospel because he or she does not trust the Body of Christ to understand it is being used by the devil to "kill" the prophets.

That is not an accomplishment I want on my heavenly résumé.

Think on This

Picture yourself, as a Jew, listening to Peter's first sermon on the first day of the Church. How might you have responded to what he said? How does God's willingness to birth His Church in the midst of a perverse generation affect your thinking about what He might do today? Is the prophetic a comfortable or uncomfortable topic for you, and why? Have you ever asked God for His insight in this area? Which Scriptures support your position? Which seem to be in conflict? What is your conclusion?

Note

1. John Phillips, *The Bible Explorer's Guide* (Grand Rapids, MI: Kregel Publications, 2002), 126.

Chapter 3

Three Revelations and Your Spiritual DNA

But as it is written: "Eye has not seen, nor ear heard, nor have entered into the heart of man the things which God has prepared for those who love Him." But God has revealed them to us through His Spirit (1 Corinthians 2:9-10).

God has prepared amazing things for us, things our physical senses cannot detect. Only the eyes and ears of faith can grasp them, and that only *through* His Spirit. That which the Holy Spirit unveils is *revelation.* We use the word freely in modern society to describe the disclosure of surprising, shocking, or titillating information. Although revelation from the Holy Spirit is often surprising and provocative, it delves deeper than human information, ideas, or even wisdom ever could.

Here is how Thayer's Lexicon defines revelation:

1) laying bare, making naked

2) a disclosure of truth, instruction a) concerning things before unknown b) used of events by which things or states or persons hitherto withdrawn from view are made visible to all

3) manifestation, appearance[1]

God gives revelation to show us Himself, produce change, and birth something new within us. Revelation opens our eyes to see things according to His truth. By revelation, we see what the human eye cannot detect. In the light of revelation, our perspectives are transformed and our preconceptions unravel. As it is activated in the heart of a believer, revelation increases spiritual maturity and dispels darkness by shedding His light. It lifts God's people above the limits of the natural world and natural thought.

Revelation powerfully impacts the identity and life of the believer. Before we dig into the subject of our spiritual DNA, we need to explore three foundational revelations—I call them the three *greatest* revelations—that form the heart of our spiritual understanding and our outcomes in life.

These three revelations are sequential. When we receive the first, we are able to grasp the second. When the second is in place, the third naturally unfolds. They are:

1. The revelation of Jesus's divinity

2. The revelation of identity

3. The revelation of destiny

When these three revelations are firmly established in our hearts, God's plan for our lives is radically facilitated. The chromosomes in our spiritual DNA begin to fire on all cylinders, bringing forth the fullness of our destinies in divine order.

Peter's Revelation

To see how these revelations work, let's follow their operation in the life of the apostle Peter. We know that Jesus spent three intense years with Peter and the rest of the disciples. The Bible records quite a few of their intimate conversations, but none is more memorable than an exchange between Jesus and Peter. It began when Jesus asked the disciples a question: *"Who do men say that I, the Son of Man, am?"* (Matt. 16:13).

Jesus was not mining for information. He already knew what had been said about Him. Instead, His question was designed to take the spiritual pulse of His disciples. All but one of them took His query at face value and offered a laundry list of answers they had heard: *"Some say* [You are] *John the Baptist, some Elijah, and others Jeremiah or one of the prophets"* (Matt. 16:14).

Jesus pressed the issue, asking, *"But who do you say that I am?"* (Matt 16:15). That is when Peter separated himself from the crowd and responded from the deeper place of revelation:

> *Simon Peter answered and said, "You are the Christ, the Son of the living God."*
>
> *Jesus answered and said to him, "Blessed are you, Simon Bar-Jonah, for flesh and blood has not revealed this to you, but My Father who is in heaven. And I also say to you that you are Peter, and on this rock I will build My church, and*

> *the gates of Hades shall not prevail against it"* (Matthew 16:16-18).

Peter's response was a game-changer. He'd heard the same scuttlebutt as everyone else, but his answer was completely different. Jesus explained what the difference was: Peter had not drawn his answer from his intellect or from the court of public opinion; he perceived the answer from something His Father in heaven unveiled—*revelation.*

The Revelation of Divinity

When Jesus asked, "Who do men say I am?" He knew exactly how His disciples would formulate their answers—which is the same way we do. We begin by accumulating information. Since we are partial to facts that can be nailed down in black and white, we then try to organize our data into neat bundles of statistics and reports that can be used to shape our assumptions and decisions. These bundles rarely stay neat, because facts on the ground are always subject to change. When they shift, our assessments shift too.

Until we base our beliefs about Jesus and ourselves on revelation, we are building our lives on the shifting sands of opinion and intellect. The world's opinions are fluid; they vary from person to person and from day to day. When our seemingly rational ideas fail to line up with what God is doing, we strain at the bit and come up with answers like, "He was John the Baptist, raised from the dead." This idea was even crazier than the truth seemed at the time, since Jesus and John were born just months apart and had been seen together in public!

You can see why Jesus pressed His question, in essence saying, "Yes, I know all about what people say; but who do *you* say that I am? What do *you* believe?"

The disciples had seen Jesus's every move. They heard His words and saw His miracles. They were firsthand witnesses to the accounts we read in the Gospels. Every one of them should have been able to say, "Without a doubt, You are the Christ."

Yet, only Peter said it—and he said it only because the Father had removed the veil from his eyes. What Peter saw was beyond his natural capacity to perceive—right before his spiritual eyes, the Father revealed the divinity of Jesus.

Faith Is Based on Revelation

In Jesus's day, most Jews knew about the Messianic prophecies. Modern Bible readers might assume, therefore, that Peter researched centuries of writings and recognized Jesus because of them. But Peter was not a scholar; he was a simple fisherman. Even the scholars whose lives were dedicated to the Scriptures and the Law did not recognize Jesus as their Messiah.

An enduring faith is not based on historical, circumstantial, or even scientific evidence. It is based on the revelation of Jesus's divinity and His saving blood. When your faith is based on revelation, *nothing* can shake it—not contrary evidence or pain, not loss or persecution. Even if all hell breaks loose in your life, you would continue in faith, blessing His name and believing that He is both Lord and Savior.

Revelation Is Progressive

Revelation is not exclusive to New Testament believers. Adam walked with God in the Garden and received understanding directly from Him. God gave Noah detailed instructions for building the ark and afterward made an eternal covenant with him. An old man named Abram received the promise of a son. It seemed an impossible pledge to keep, but God kept it anyway.

Over time, God has revealed Himself and His plans progressively, in part through His descriptive names. In Genesis, He was Elohim, the great and glorious Creator. To Abraham, He was El Shaddai, the One who was more than enough to make the impossible possible by bringing forth a son from the "dead" body of an old man and his wife's dead womb (see Rom. 4:19).

All of the patriarchs received direct revelation from God. Yet, in Exodus 6:3, God told Moses, *"I appeared to Abraham, to Isaac, and to Jacob, as God Almighty, but by My name Lord* [Yahweh, or Jehovah] *I was not known to them."*

In Moses's mind, Abraham, Isaac, and Jacob were the patriarchal gold standard. Yet Moses got to know God in a way that his predecessors had not. Now the people needed Moses's new revelation. They had to know the changeless *I AM* who would lead them through the wilderness and into the Promised Land. They had to know the immoveable, unchangeable God who would keep them whole, watch their backs, and care for their every need.

In Exodus 6:6-7, God told Moses to share the revelation of Jehovah, the One for whom Pharaoh would be no match. This Jehovah later *"came down in a cloud and stood there with* [Moses]; *and He called out His own name, Yahweh....the God of compassion and mercy...slow to anger and filled with unfailing love and faithfulness"* (Exod. 34:5-6 NLT).

Just as God encouraged Abraham, He continually spoke to Moses. He revealed Himself by the names that addressed

Israel's needs, in real time. They got to know Him as Jehovah Rapha ("God my Healer"), Jehovah Nissi ("God my Banner"), and Jehovah M'Kaddesh ("God who Sanctifies").[2]

The revelation of God's born-again people exceeds even that which Moses enjoyed. Now, the Spirit of God lives inside us and we are His temple. We know that Jesus is the Christ, the Redeemer. His Holy Spirit bears witness with our spirit that we are His children (see Rom. 8:16). Moses could not claim such revelation as God offers us!

Revelation is not based in statistics or scientific proof, yet it is partly relational and experiential. Through the trials of life, we discover new aspects of God, just as the Israelites did—things we did not recognize before the struggle exposed it.

The Martha and Mary Revelation

The death and resurrection of Jesus's friend Lazarus is a stunning example of how God reveals Himself through adversity. When Jesus received word that His good friend Lazarus was sick, He delayed going to the man's aid.

> [Jesus] *said, "This sickness is not unto death, but for the glory of God, that the Son of God may be glorified through it." Now Jesus loved Martha and her sister and Lazarus. So, when He heard that* [Lazarus] *was sick, He stayed two more days in the place where He was* (John 11:4-6).

At best, Jesus's decision seems counterintuitive. As far as Lazarus's family could tell, its consequences were fatal. By the time Jesus reached Lazarus, he was dead and buried. His sisters, Martha and Mary, were disappointed; they expected Jesus to come quickly and heal their brother while his heart was still beating. Martha told it like she saw it: *"Lord, if You had been here, my brother would not have died"* (John 11:21).

Lazarus's family had faith in Jesus. They knew Him as the Healer. They believed that if Jesus had shown up on time, Lazarus would still be alive. Jesus, however, intended to disclose something more about who He was. Knowing the Healer was important; but knowing the Resurrection and the Life had greater eternal consequences. Jesus pressed the issue in His conversation with Martha:

> *Jesus said to* [Martha], *"Your brother will rise again."*
>
> *Martha said to Him, "I know that he will rise again in the resurrection at the last day."*
>
> *Jesus said to her,* ***"I am the resurrection and the life. He who believes in Me, though he may die, he shall live. And whoever lives and believes in Me shall never die.*** *Do you believe this?"*
>
> *She said to Him, "Yes, Lord, I believe that You are the Christ, the Son of God, who is to come into the world"* (John 11:23-27).

While Martha lamented what might have been, Jesus pointed her toward what could be. As she and Mary dwelt on their brother's seemingly unnecessary death, Jesus prepared their hearts for a transformational revelation that would shatter their limited paradigm and heighten their faith.

Had Jesus arrived while Lazarus was still alive, the sisters' faith would have topped off at the level of Jesus the Healer.

They would have missed the massive growth spurt He had in mind. His delay in coming to their aid was *for the sake of their faith.* That is why He told His disciples beforehand: *"I am glad for your sakes that I was not there, that you may believe"* (John 11:15). Another version translates His statement this way: *"I'm glad that I wasn't there so that you can* ***grow in faith****"* (GW).

Jesus planned to release a higher revelation of His divinity, but a higher level of faith would be needed to receive it. Allowing His good friend to die would allow this spiritual stretching to occur. Clearly, only Jesus knew that Lazarus would live again. The sisters and all who had gathered saw nothing ahead but mourning. Instead, they witnessed the unimaginable—resurrection life. Now they could believe God for *anything.*

The Revelation of Identity

If there is a single statement that encapsulates my ministry as a pastor and prophet it is the one I have repeated countless times over the decades: *You are who God says you are.* Let me warn you that if you are not careful, you will see these seven words as a saccharine-laced catchphrase that pastors and other Christians spout when they can't think of anything more spiritual to say.

That misunderstanding could cost you more than you want to pay. Knowing who God says you are means knowing what Jesus died to give you—and it is more than forgiveness from sin. When a person is born again, regeneration occurs. I've heard T.D. Jakes pronounce it rē·GĒNE·er·ation. And that is exactly what it is! When salvation is received, a person's spiritual DNA is re-created. Instead of reflecting the genetics and limitations of the natural bloodline, the new DNA comes from the perfect, most pristine source of all: the divine gene pool!

Salvation's vast eternal ramifications are indisputable. Yet God knew forgiveness was not enough. In order for us to live forgiven, we need an identity overhaul—the kind of transformation that turned Jacob, the supplanter, into *Israel,* the one who "will rule as God." A similar remapping of identity turned Saul, the murderer of Christians, into Paul, the Christ-lover assigned to share the revelation of God's grace with all of Christendom and the world.

Salvation produces more than a community of new "creatures"; it transforms us into entirely new creations.

A divine identity overhaul would result from the conversation between Jesus and Peter in Matthew 16. Peter's revelation of the Christ and Jesus's validation of the source of the revelation (see Matt. 16–17) began a chain of events that would cleanse and revitalize Peter's thinking and empower him to see himself differently. With the divinity issue settled, Jesus unveiled Peter's true identity, saying, *"You are Peter, and on this rock I will build My church, and the gates of Hades shall not prevail against it"* (Matt. 16:18).

When we recognize Jesus's divinity, we can receive the revelation of who we are in God's eyes. We are just like Peter—we label ourselves according to our circumstances, occupations, and tendencies. We see ourselves as being poor or well-to-do. We call ourselves mothers, breadwinners, fisherman, doctors, preachers, or accountants. We affix labels that identify us as being gifted, shy, athletic, or insecure. But when we learn who God is, we discover who we *really* are. Peter was known as a fisherman and small businessman, an impulsive and mercurial character who talked first and thought later.

But God saw much more. Peter would be one of the Church's original apostles. He was slated to become a pivotal figure in the soon-coming Church. When Jesus blessed Simon Bar-Jonah and said, "You are Peter," He activated Peter's future. In essence, He said: "I know you see yourself as a fisherman who is following the Christ, but I have even bigger plans for you. You are 'the rock.' You cannot fully understand this new name yet, but you will in time. For now, know this: You are who *I* say you are. When the time comes, you will be ready for what I have planned."

When God reveals His divinity, we can detect our spiritual DNA. Even if Peter nursed his self-concept as a fisherman who was too rough around the edges to be anything else, he had seen enough to know there was more ahead. Revelation pressed him forward and into his undeniable and rightful place in the Church.

If you know Jesus is the Christ and you have accepted His sacrifice, you too have enough revelation to take your place in God's plan. Are you willing to accept God's assessment of who you are? Are you willing to release yourself from the name *Simon Bar-Jonah* and become the *Peter* He is revealing? Will you drop your misgivings and trust Him as Peter did?

Your divine DNA was engineered to supersede the circumstances of your natural life. If you are born again, you are not who you once were. If you have accepted Jesus's sacrifice, you have been spiritually "transfused." Your bloodline and blood type were changed for eternity. Whatever earthly curse was genetically passed down to you—drug abuse, heart disease, depression, or cancer—it is no longer part of your makeup. You have been regenerated! Your very life is found in *His* blood, not yours (see Lev. 17:11).

PROPHETIC PERSPECTIVE

Unless you have a prophetic perspective, your past is the only foundation upon which you can base your future. Once you are born again, however, you can say, "I am who I am because of the blood that was shed for me and the Holy Spirit who lives within me. I have been redeemed and regenerated and I know who I am in Christ. The person I used to be is dead, gone, and buried. The real me has arrived and I'm ready for my future."

THE REVELATION OF DESTINY

Have you ever heard people, especially young people, say that they are trying to find themselves? The problem they are having is less about finding themselves than it is about finding Him. Once you discover His divinity, you find your spiritual DNA. And with your DNA settled, you will know where you are going.

Once Peter recognized the divinity of Jesus, he found himself. That does not mean he had it all together or everything worked out perfectly for the rest of his life. The man Jesus called "the rock" denied Him three times and returned to the fishing business after the resurrection. Yet, as far as God was concerned, Peter would always be "the rock." His failings could not change his spiritual DNA.

One of Peter's enduring qualities was his knack for being first: he was the first and only disciple to walk on water, the first to receive the revelation of Jesus's divinity, the first to receive the revelation of his own spiritual identity, the first to preach a sermon in the new Church of Jesus Christ, and the facilitator of the first Gentile revival (see Acts 10). But Peter did not cook up these circumstances of his life and ministry. He did not ask to become "the rock" or to be the first at anything. His spiritual destiny was God's idea. Peter's role in the launching and maturing of the Church had been activated before he knew what his role was. He simply answered Jesus's question with the revelation the Father had given him; and Jesus did the rest.

Peter's identity had already been settled in heaven. It was directly connected to his kingdom destiny. When Jesus pulled him out of the water (see Matt. 14:31), He rescued more than a fisherman—He rescued "the rock."

Connected to Life

Peter's life, much like yours, was not connected to self but to every word that proceeds from the mouth of God. Everything Peter accomplished began with a word from God. The revelation of the Christ had proceeded from the mouth of God to Peter's spiritual ears (see Matt. 16:17). Even Peter's walk on water was inspired by Jesus's word, *"Come"* (Matt. 14:29). Peter took what Jesus said to heart; therefore, he believed he could do the impossible.

We are quick to attribute all that we are to a family tree, a cultural background, the right education (or lack thereof), or the kind of upbringing we received. We see ourselves as the clinical product of sperm and egg. Too easily we accept the natural outcomes of life because we believe they are dictated by our physical DNA and past history.

I am here to tell you that there is something far more important than where you came from or how you were conceived. Your spiritual DNA is supernaturally charged to override your physical makeup. The person you really are came from more than the physical union of your biological parents. The real you—the person encoded in your spiritual DNA—was created by the proceeding word of God.

God's plan for you did not begin in your mother's womb or the delivery room; it began in eternity with Him. The prophet Jeremiah received this revelation centuries ago when God explained his roots: *"Before I formed you in the womb I knew you; before you were born I sanctified you; I ordained you a prophet to the nations"* (Jer. 1:5).

God "conceived" Jeremiah before his parents came together. Of course, God uses our natural circumstances. His Word says *"that **all** things work together for good to those who love God, to those who are the called according to His purpose"* (Rom. 8:28). But God's idea of our individual identities and destinies will never be limited by our physical or biological makeup.

When God told Abram that he would be the father of a great nation, the appointment was not based on Abram's family heritage. He was born beyond the Euphrates, where his father, Terah, worshiped other gods (see Gen. 12:2; 15:5; 17:4; Josh. 24:2;14-15). When God called David to be the next king of Israel, it was not on the basis of David's stature or maturity. His older brother Eliab seemed more suitable in that regard (see 1 Sam. 16:12-13;6-7). When Jesus called Peter "the rock," his reputation was anything but solid; he was a chronically fickle and changeable man.

These men's destinies were not connected to self, but to a *God said*.

Every chaos-reversing, darkness-defying word from God stamps your DNA with His vision for your life. It is not surprising that the enemy works so furiously to void these heavenly transactions! He will pound away at your *God said* and say, "You are nothing! You'll go nowhere. You will never amount to anything!"

Let me give you an ironclad defense against this demonic tactic: Many outstanding men and women in the Bible came from "nothing." David was a shepherd boy, Ruth was a poor Moabitess, and Gideon came from a puny family. Yet, with a personal, proceeding word from God, each rose far above the level of their circumstances. Their losses were reversed, their reputations were elevated, and they accomplished great things for God.

God's heroes and heroines have never fit the world's idea of eligibility. Outwardly, they do not look like prize packages. They are ordinary people who are humble enough to be transformed by His speaking. They are willing to submit to the voice of God that shakes natural circumstances and unleashes transformation. Just as natural sperm and egg unite to produce physical DNA, so the spiritual chromosomes of God's people are created when His word collides with the measure of faith all of us have received (see Rom. 12:3).

The moment you hear God's proceeding word and receive it by faith, your spiritual DNA is birthed and your destiny is activated. Regardless of your past experiences and the continued depersonalization of modern culture, you are more than a "has been" or a number. You are a human being with a promising destiny in God and a fingerprint all your own. There will never be another *you.*

Seeing or Believing?

When I began in ministry, my father gave me sound advice: "Son, pray for two things every day—wisdom and the spirit of revelation." As a teenager with a hunger to serve God, I understood his advice only in part. As I matured, however, I understood that Dad was telling me that God could literally strip the scales off my spiritual eyes, heal the deafness of my spiritual ears, and transform my carnal mind so that I would become *"subject to the law of God"* (Rom. 8:7).

God is not looking for know-it-alls. I am living proof of that. But He will work through those who seek revelation directly from His heart to theirs. It does not matter how much data they have amassed or how impressive their résumés are. What matters is their willingness to rely on whatever the Holy Spirit reveals.

If you are a preacher, you can preach the greatest sermon since the Day of Pentecost, but unless revelation by the Holy Spirit is involved, your words will fall to the ground. It does not matter how many miracles can be attributed to your ministry. Even if amputees sprout new limbs when you pray, your ministry will be proven hollow without revelation.

Carnal methods cannot convince people to walk with Christ. Only the convicting and revealing work of the Holy Spirit can cause a man or woman to accept the Savior. His work in us is the basis of our faith. The world sees it differently. The world says, "Seeing is believing." They could not be more wrong. First of all, people do not always believe what they see. How many people watched Jesus raise the dead and open blind eyes, and still called for Him to be crucified?

Spiritually speaking, believing is seeing, because faith is what enables us to see. Still, we must hunger for revelation to see all that God has prepared for us. Not everyone—not even every Christian—hungers in this way. This is in part why Paul quoted from the Old Testament in his letter to the Corinthians, *"Eye has not seen, nor ear heard, nor have entered into the heart of man the things which God has prepared for those who love Him"* (1 Cor. 2:9).

Much of the world has been trained to suppress this hunger to the point that they disdain spiritual things. They seek to disprove miracles and deny the power and presence of God. Yet, when catastrophes occur—when tsunamis sweep people out to sea or tornadoes level cities—they are quick to blame Him. They come loaded with pat answers about how the world works, but if you ask them to explain the resurrection and the historical evidence of its occurrence, they cannot.

When it comes right down to it, you either have a revelation of Christ or you don't.

A Male Child and a Prophet

How I thank God for the example and testimony of my parents, who held unswervingly to God's heart! They hungered to hear His voice; and when they did, they became one with whatever He said, no matter the cost.

When I was in my mother's womb, God spoke to both my parents. He simply said, "The child being carried is a male child, and he shall be a prophet to My people."

This happened before the days of prenatal ultrasound. Nobody knew the sex of a child until it was born. Nevertheless, my parents planned for the birth of a boy. They had heard from God and were convinced of what He'd said. When the day of my birth came, my father paced in the waiting room of the maternity ward with the other fathers-to-be. Husbands had not been invited into delivery rooms in those days, so they just waited for the news.

While my father paced, the nurse asked him the customary question: "What will you name your baby?"

Dad said, "The baby will be named Mark Timothy."

The nurse asked, "What if it's a girl?"

My father replied, "It will not be a girl."

"So, you don't have a girl's name picked out?" she asked.

"No ma'am, we don't. His name shall be Mark Timothy."

My father was nearly 6' 5" and had silver hair. He was an imposing, John Wayne type of character. Irritating him was not the smartest thing you could do, but the nurse persisted. She told my father, "Well, there's a 50/50 chance your baby will be a girl. What are you going to do if it is?"

I can picture my father's face when he answered: "We will send the baby back, because God said it will be a male, he will be a prophet to His people, and his name shall be Mark Timothy!"

Neither the nurse nor I had any say in this. God had spoken and that was that. My folks had no back-up plan, no female names just in case, and no contingencies for any outcome other than the one God had revealed. This confidence was also transferred to my life. I understood from childhood that God had a specific destiny and purpose for my life, and I began moving in the prophetic shortly after receiving the baptism of the Holy Spirit. I was just 13 or 14 years old and had a lot of spiritual development ahead of me. Yet, the manifestation of what God prophesied was underway.

> *"For the gifts and the calling of God are irrevocable"* (Romans 11:29).

My prophetic identity was established before my birth and it continues to unfold today. In 1970, I preached my first evangelistic crusade. Although I was not quite 16, I already had a reputation for an accurate prophetic gift.

Today, I am a pastor and a prophet. Everything about our church, Word of Life Christian Center (WOLCC), is cut from the same prophetic cloth as I am. There is no escaping it—for WOLCC or for me. I admit that at times, I tried to soften my prophetic edge, but it was useless. Our church was birthed to proclaim and demonstrate, not to be cute or seeker-sensitive. God has called me to cry aloud and spare not. He gave me a voice like a trumpet and words that strike like a hammer (see Isa. 58:1; Jer. 23:29). Our spiritual DNA was activated by God, not us.

Multigenerational Prophetic Anointing

My prophetic identity is part of a multigenerational transfer. My father had a strong prophetic anointing that many in our church remember well. The generational thread was always clear, but never as clear as when I preached in San Francisco a number of years ago.

The meeting was at a church my father once pastored. As I ministered, I was prompted by the Holy Spirit to call out the pastor's wife and another woman, the church administrator. The pastor, his wife, and the administrator had all gotten saved and filled with the Holy Spirit under my father's ministry.

When the women listened to the CDs of what I prophesied over them, they discovered what I could not have known: my father had prophesied to them some 40 years earlier, when prophecies were recorded by someone with a pen and a notepad. They compared the new prophecies with the notes from 40 years ago. Everything I said under the unction of the Holy Spirit was exactly what my father had spoken—word for word!

So why did God repeat Himself? He not only confirmed and reaffirmed His earlier words, but He spoke them again, when the timing had become especially relevant for the women. Only God could have produced such a completely supernatural result.

Junkyard Vision

I said earlier that God uses whatever means necessary to reveal Himself. The same is true when He reveals our identities and destinies. God's disclosure in these areas is weighty because they involve His eternal purpose, which also involves the destinies of many people and even nations. Yet, more often than not, believers shelve these revelations, often indefinitely.

A few years ago, God gave me a vision that speaks to this issue. He showed me a junkyard. But instead of being littered with broken-down cars and auto parts, it was stacked with crosses, each cross bearing a name. The sight was so unusual, so I asked, "God, what does this mean?"

He answered, "This is the place of abandoned calls."

His answer hit me hard. I realized immediately why Jesus said, *"The harvest truly is plentiful, but the laborers are few"* (Matt. 9:37). The laborers are few because so many people disconnect from the revelation that unlocks identity and destiny. Then when stress and trouble come, they think, "The call wasn't real. I must have made it up in my own head." They abandon the call before they even begin.

Jesus said, *"If anyone desires to come after Me, let him deny himself, and take up his cross daily, and follow Me"* (Luke 9:23). The cross was Jesus's call. It was the reason He came to earth as a Man. We are not called to be crucified—but the cross each of us carries is the call of God. When He said, "Take up your cross," He was saying, "Take up your destiny, your calling, and follow Me."

We abandon the call when we lack the revelation to sustain it. We drop our crosses in the junkyard when our careers or immoral relationships derail us. We let go of God's vision when we take the path of least resistance by trading the meat of God's Word for milk and trading intimacy with God for the convenience of our own ways.

The reality is that no matter how early we abandon our callings or how far we try to run from the junkyard, we cannot escape His call. I am not suggesting that it is easy to fulfill your destiny. If it were, everyone would be doing it. Yet, as tough as it is to follow through, it is far easier to carry your cross than to bear the lifelong absence of divine purpose.

There is no doubt that we must reach the lost. But I am convinced that we must also reach our AWOL brothers and sisters. They are wandering through life and wondering their way through the emptiness. They need restoration and we need them to return to the field of battle. God has not forgotten the calls He issued them. He stands ready to reconnect them with their divine destinies.

Spiritual DNA: Prophetically Activated and Eternal

The release of the prophetic transmits the DNA of your spiritual identity and destiny. Both are connected to a *God said.* Because God is not flaky, forgetful, or fickle, your *God said* does not change or expire.

The story of the Moabite king Balak and the soothsayer Balaam reveals God's steadfastness in upholding His words (see Num. 22–24). Balak feared the Israelites and hired Balaam to curse them. The seer tried repeatedly to satisfy the king's orders, but could not. Because God had already blessed His people, even Balaam's attempted curses came out as blessings!

The king was furious. Balaam was an unholy man, yet he had already warned the king that God's word would stand. Now he repeated his admonishment: *"Did I not tell you, saying, 'All that the Lord speaks, that I must do'?"* (Num. 23:26).

God called Israel *blessed*; therefore she could not be cursed. Even though Israel had repeatedly fallen into idolatry, God never rescinded His blessing. Israel is fruitful and strong to this day, despite the fact that she is literally surrounded by enemies and has been attacked mercilessly throughout history.

When God speaks, He prophesies. Your *God said* is a strong anchor. It will hold you steady in rough seas. It will defy contrary circumstances. It will guide you through transition, and undergird your victory. Even when your situation seems diametrically opposed to what God promised, His proceeding word will not falter.

Peter described the power and trustworthiness of God's speaking, saying, *"And so we have the prophetic word confirmed, which you do well to heed as a light that shines in a dark place, until the day dawns and the morning star rises in your hearts"* (2 Pet. 1:19).

Are you in a season of drought? Has everything that you treasure seemed to dry up? I know how devastating that can be, but I can assure you without hesitation that your *God said* is still alive. Even at the height of scarcity and loss, God will reposition you for the kind of breakthrough you could not have experienced when life seemed rosy.

The same Joel who prophesied the outpouring of the Holy Spirit acknowledged the reality of scarcity. The Book of Joel begins with an assessment of the worst of times already experienced and yet to come:

> *The word of the Lord that came to Joel the son of Pethuel. Hear this, you elders, and give ear, all you inhabitants of the land! Has anything like this happened in your days, or even in the days of your fathers? Tell your children about it, let your children tell their children, and their children another generation. What the chewing locust left, the swarming locust has eaten; what the swarming*

> *locust left, the crawling locust has eaten; and what the crawling locust left, the consuming locust has eaten* (Joel 1:1-4).

Of course Joel's prophecy did not end there. In the 2nd chapter of Joel, just before his description of Pentecost and beyond, he prophesied restoration!

> *So I will restore to you the years that the swarming locust has eaten, the crawling locust, the consuming locust, and the chewing locust* (Joel 2:25).

I firmly believe that if you will stand firm in these difficult times and cling to your *God said* without compromise, you will experience a breathtaking restoration. You and others will marvel, saying, "How did this happen so suddenly? How could this situation turn around overnight?"

Get ready, dear friend, for your spiritual DNA is already working, and your destiny awaits you.

Think on This

What discrepancies are apparent between your *God said* and your life outcomes to date? What conclusions have you drawn about this in the past? How do your conclusions reflect, or fail to reflect, the reality of the three revelations? What new revelation is God offering and how does it affect your identity and destiny?

Notes

1. *Blue Letter Bible,* Dictionary and Word Search for *"apokalypsis"* (Strong's 602), Blue Letter Bible, 1996-2011,

http://www.blueletterbible.org/lang/lexicon/lexicon.cfm ?Strongs=G602&t=KJV (accessed November 26, 2011).

2. See Exodus 15:26; 17:15; Leviticus 20:8.

Chapter 4

Profile of a Prophetic People

But you are a chosen generation, a royal priesthood, a holy nation, His own special people, that you may proclaim the praises of Him who called you out of darkness into His marvelous light (1 Peter 2:9).

The call out of darkness and into His light is both wonderful and weighty. Through no merit of our own, and only by way of His righteousness, we have been given God's perfect promises. That is the wonderful part of being called out of darkness. The weighty part is that we are called to authenticity, balance, and accountability. God's prophetic generation knows the difference between His holy fire and an emotionally-generated hot flash. We seek Him and His proceeding word, not the latest "buzz" or prophetic flavor of the month.

God's prophetic generation displays its spiritual profile amid an age so twisted that it turns the stomach. Yet, perversion is nothing new. The current age is the distant cousin of the adulterous and wicked one Jesus addressed in the Gospels. The world's fallen nature is nothing new; while its condition might disgust us, it is no hindrance to God.

The Word became flesh *in the midst of depravity.* That should inspire hope. Although the decay we see is real, we know that wherever sin abounds, grace abounds much more (see Rom. 5:20). God's prophetic generation operates in that grace to be salt and light to humankind. This is not an assignment for one man or one woman; it is up to a people to reveal the Restorer of the Breach (see Isa. 58:12).

Many trustworthy leaders in the Body of Christ are doing their part, yet none of them is called to possess the territory singlehandedly: *"God is with the* ***generation*** *of the righteous"* (Ps. 14:5). Even in ancient times, God needed more than one leader to fulfill His plan. He told Joshua, *"Arise, go over this Jordan,* ***you and all this people,*** *to the land which I am giving to them—the children of Israel"* (Josh. 1:2). It takes a generation to possess the promise.

Generation Basics

The word *generation* is used in many ways. It can refer to a group of people born during a particular period of time (such as Generation X) or to an actual time span (such as the Vietnam War era). The word can also denote a group of likeminded people, such as the hippie generation. The Hebrew word *dowr* (translated "generation" in Psalm 14:5), captures these meanings, and more:

1) period, generation, habitation, dwelling

a) period, age, generation (period of time)

b) generation (those living during a period)

c) generation (characterised by quality, condition, class of men)

d) dwelling-place, habitation[1]

Whatever the application of the word, every generation is distinct. Nevertheless, all generations share three basic characteristics:

- *Every generation has a father or fathers.* Fathers usher in the next generation and leave a legacy for their progeny to carry forward. Fathers have great power to affect the future.
- *Every generation of people is distinct.* Each has its own story and, therefore, its own outcomes. Generation Xers don't think the way Baby Boomers do, and Millennials see things differently than Xers. Each generation's unique experience produces an equally individual mindset.
- *Every era is distinct.* Time periods are also easily distinguished. The World War II era and the 1960s were radically different. Both were marked by war, yet perceptions of the Vietnam War were radically different from those of WWII. As a result, the Vietnam War era literally transformed the political, cultural, and philosophical landscape of the time.

The Nature of God's Prophetic Generation

A prophetic generation is, by nature, a hungry generation. I am not talking about those whose stomachs growl during Sunday service. A prophetic generation is hungry for God, for a move of God, for His presence, and for righteousness. They hunger in the *now*. They are not satisfied to imagine what God will do someday. They peer into His heart and ask, "What are You doing now, Lord? How can I be a part of it?"

Prophetic generations are not willing to be passed over. They don't live on the sidelines; they long to be at the epicenter of whatever God is doing. They are the rare Enochs—people who walk with God at a level of intimacy others are unwilling to pursue (see Gen. 5:23-24; Heb. 11:5).

The motto of a prophetic people is *"seek first the kingdom of God and His righteousness, and all these things shall be added to you"* (Matt. 6:33). They are proactive and on the offense. God is raising them up to be warriors. They are people with a backbone who are willing to risk it all for Him. They do not seek to be popular or coddled. They are not dull of hearing or spiritually blind. They are opposite to those described by Paul when he quoted Isaiah:

> *For the hearts of this people have grown dull. Their ears are hard of hearing, and their eyes they have closed, lest they should see with their eyes and hear with their ears, lest they should understand with their hearts and turn, so that I should heal them* (Acts 28:27; see Isaiah 6:9-10).

Isaiah's quote did not describe a prophetic people. The generation I am talking about consists of those who are receptive to God's Word and never ashamed of the Gospel. They understand that it is *"the power of God unto salvation to every one that believeth"* (Rom. 1:16 KJV).

God's prophetic people love truth. They are like the Bereans who weighed all they heard against the Word of God (see Acts 17:11). Unlike the faithless generation described in Second Timothy 4:3-4, this righteous generation endures sound doctrine and turns away from ear-tickling fables. They are a blessed people *"who hunger and thirst for righteousness"* (Matt. 5:6).

Characteristics of a Prophetic People

Remember that the Church was birthed as God's prophetic vehicle. So the question is not whether we are called to be a prophetic people, but whether we choose to walk in the calling. Now that we have seen the big picture in regard to the prophetic profile, let's look at specific attributes of the prophetic generation.

They Are a Proclaiming People

"In the beginning was the Word, and the Word was with God, and the Word was God" (John 1:1). Individually and collectively, the Word is our foundation and sustenance. It leads us to salvation and into all of God's will. Words are meant to be spoken; therefore, God's prophetic generation is necessarily a proclaiming generation.

Romans 10:14-15 explains:

> *How then shall they call on Him in whom they have not believed? And how shall they believe in*

> *Him of whom they have not heard? And how shall they hear without a preacher? And how shall they preach unless they are sent? As it is written: "How beautiful are the feet of those who preach the gospel of peace, who bring glad tidings of good things!"*

The Gospel is shared and received by speaking and hearing. As a proclaiming people, we boldly declare that we do not live by bread alone, but by every word that proceeds from the mouth of God (see Deut. 8:3). We verbalize only what is in agreement with what God says. God's prophetic generation does not replicate the example of the ten spies who surveyed the Promised Land and discouraged the Israelites from taking it (see Num. 13–14).

A prophetic people follow the model of Joshua and Caleb, who aligned themselves with God's promise—they open their mouths and truth spills out. Today's Joshuas and Calebs are warriors whose *"loins* [are] *girt about with truth"* (Eph. 6:14 KJV). Spiritually speaking, the loins are the warriors' words—life-giving, yoke-destroying words. God's truth is an offensive weapon that demolishes demonic schemes and brings life to people's destinies.

> *"Death and life are in the power of the tongue..."* (Proverbs 18:21).

God's prophetic generation cannot help but proclaim His truth. Because He used words, not just to predict, but also to create all that exists, God's people also create with their words. This creativity is not reserved for the pulpit alone. The pulpit is assigned to propagate the spiritual maturity that causes believers to speak as oracles of God. Everyone in God's prophetic generation is called to proclaim—in the workplace, the family, the schools, and the government.

They Edify, Exhort, and Comfort Others

God's prophetic generation has a specific biblical mandate: to speak *"edification and exhortation and comfort to men"* (1 Cor. 14:3). Whenever and wherever God's Word is proclaimed, it accomplishes these aims.

To edify, exhort, and comfort others, we will have to rise up out of our own sorrows, our own life dramas, our own disappointments and dysfunction. This means living beyond an "us four and no more" mentality. It requires a heart that says:

> "I have a word on my lips that can help this person. It will dispel their darkness and water their dry places. This word will create an overflow where lack exists. I may have trouble enough of my own, but my mouth is filled with words of life. He has given me a *God said* for someone and I must proclaim it!"

Paul said that in the midst of a crooked and perverse generation, we shine as lights in the world (see Phil. 2:15). A prophetic generation delivers words of life in checkout lines, in doctors' offices, and at PTA meetings—not by making religious-sounding statements or quoting Scripture in the King's English, but by speaking God's heart into every situation so that edification, exhortation, and comfort are sown into people's hearts.

When God uses you in this way, it will always be effective. People might not see your conversation as being spiritual; they might not even understand that God is involved. Yet, they will walk away thinking, "I like being around him," or "I'm always encouraged after I leave her."

Here is one more thought (for now) about the role of edification, exhortation, and comfort: Prophetic people do not come to church to receive momentary emotional boosts. They come to the house of God to be strengthened, so they *"may be able to comfort those who are in any trouble, with the comfort with which* [they themselves] *are comforted by God"* (2 Cor. 1:4).

They Are People of Action

God's prophetic people are not sloths or procrastinators. They perceive and position themselves to act, not when action is convenient or comfortable, but when it is timely and serves God's purposes.

The story of the 12 spies reveals Joshua and Caleb as prophetic proclaimers *and* as people of action. Consider the context of the story: The Israelites had been enslaved for more than 400 years. Until the spies' expedition was dispatched, no living Israelite had seen the Promised Land. All they knew about it was what God told them: it was a land of milk and honey, and it was theirs for the taking. Before the spies' report was given, the Israelites had no physical confirmation of God's promise.

Now they had eyewitness accounts that what God had been telling them was true. Even the ten admitted it, saying, *"We went to the land where you sent us.* ***It truly flows with milk and honey****"* (Num. 13:27). They brought samples of Canaan's lush, oversized fruit, and *still* the people focused on the news about the giants in the land (see Num. 13:32-33).

But Caleb saw things differently. He *"quieted the people before Moses, and said,* ***'Let us go up at once and take possession,*** *for we are well able to overcome it'"* (Num. 13:30). As far as Caleb was concerned, God could not and would not lie. Although Joshua and Caleb could not change the minds of their generation, God used them to preserve the next generation, the group that would cross the Jordan under Joshua's leadership. Of the millions who left Egypt, Joshua and Caleb were the only two who entered the Promised Land!

Prophetic people of action cannot be held down by naysayers, adversity, strong enemies, or any other form of opposition. Their default position is, "We will overcome, no matter what 'they' think...no matter what 'they' say. This is what God said, and we're *doing* it."

They Are a Claiming People

God's prophetic generation operates in confident trust because they speak only what God says. They hear God's promises and lay personal claim to them. This was true of Joshua and Caleb. They rested in what God promised, and they were determined to take the territory, not on the basis of their own strength, but because they trusted Him to back up their claim.

Notice how they responded to the defeatist report of the other ten spies:

> *But Joshua the son of Nun and Caleb the son of Jephunneh, who were among those who had spied out the land, tore their clothes; and they spoke*

> *to all the congregation of the children of Israel, saying: "The land we passed through to spy out is an exceedingly good land.* ***If the Lord delights in us, then He will bring us into this land and give it to us, 'a land which flows with milk and honey.'*** *Only do not rebel against the Lord, nor fear the people of the land, for they are our bread; their protection has departed from them, and the Lord is with us. Do not fear them"* (Numbers 14:6-9).

Joshua and Caleb were ready to claim the territory. The sight of giants in the land or the negativity surrounding them did not sway them. The ten spies chose the opposite position: They were unmoved by God's truth. He told them the land was good and it was theirs. Instead of being thankful, they whined. Their reactions were driven by emotion—specifically, fear. They wanted the lush crops, but only if they did not have to fight for them.

We are tempted every day to do the same thing. Our expectations become skewed and we see opposition as a negation of the promise. We want God to hand us His promises on a silver platter, but He wants us to stand up for them, trusting that He is backing us and them.

Your promised land might not roll out the red carpet or greet you with a "Welcome" sign. More than likely, you will have to cross a battlefield to claim it. But remember this: the battle is the Lord's and victory is assured when you stick with Him.

They Are Unmoved by Majority Opinions

Popular opinion does not motivate a prophetic people. The ten spies formed a consensus, and an entire population bought into their account. Unfortunately, they had agreed to a deception. The majority of Israelites agreed with the ten spies, but they were *wrong.*

The Israelites' wilderness experience was proof of God's faithfulness. Without Him, millions would have perished in the desert. Yet they discounted His ability to preserve them in the Promised Land. Even their firsthand, against-all-odds experiences did not convince the fearful of God's intent and integrity. They reported with dread, *"The land through which we have gone as spies is a land that devours its inhabitants"* (Num. 13:32).

The majority spoke and offered an easy out: they would forfeit the promise and avoid risking a confrontation with the giants. Joshua and Caleb rejected the people's pessimism and held to their *God said.*

Prophetic people are willing to push back against popular opinion, whatever the cost. As a pastor, I could choose an easier road than the one I am on. I could appeal to the masses by preaching motivational messages that avoid mention of the blood and the cross. However, proclaiming and doing what the Holy Spirit leads has to always outweigh the wishes of the majority.

> *"Forever, O Lord, Your word is settled in heaven"* (Psalm 119:89).

They Never Relinquish Their Spiritual Identities

Israel's willingness to forfeit the Promised Land was largely an identity problem. Their very own words revealed this: *"There we saw the giants (the descendants of Anak came from the giants);*

*and **we were like grasshoppers in our own sight,** and so we were in their sight"* (Num. 13:33).

For centuries, God had called Israel a blessed people who would bless the world (see Gen. 12:3; 28:14). After 400 years of slavery, Israel's sense of identity was so damaged that the people trash-talked themselves! For God's prophetic generation to see the fulfillment of His plans, we must remain in firm agreement with His declaration that we are *"a chosen generation, a royal priesthood, a holy nation, His own special people"* (1 Pet. 2:9).

Your personal identity in Christ does not rest on your circumstances. Whether you have money in the bank or just lost your home, whether you are facing a "giant" on the job or in your health, you are *His.* You were not born in this season by accident but by divine design. He imprinted your spiritual DNA with a specific destiny which He will not revoke. *You are no grasshopper.*

Do not lay your identity down in the face of intimidation. Do not relinquish it through self-defeating attitudes and words. Disregard the negative assessments of those who say, "You'll never amount to anything," or "You're dreaming too big." Remember that your identity and your destiny are inseparable; to lay down one is to surrender the other.

Do you remember what Paul told his protégé Timothy? He said, *"This charge I commit to you, son Timothy, according to the prophecies previously made concerning you, that by them you may wage the good warfare"* (1 Tim. 1:18). Paul reminded Timothy about the prophecies that had been spoken over him because these *God saids* revealed aspects of Timothy's identity and destiny.

When you know who you are and what you were created to do, you have mighty weapons to wield against the enemy. In the midst of calamity, you can rise up and say, "I am who God says I am; therefore, I will do what He called me to do. You are a liar, devil, and I *refuse* to become your grasshopper."

They Do Not Murmur

Have you ever noticed that self-defeating, self-sabotaging people like to murmur and complain? Even though God promised the Israelites a swath of prime real estate, miraculously delivered them from enslavement, and revealed Himself through staggering signs and wonders, the Israelites felt "less than" the godless giants of Canaan.

Small-minded and self-focused, the Israelites nitpicked at every turn and cried out to return to Egypt:

> *And all the children of Israel murmured against Moses and against Aaron: and the whole congregation said unto them, Would God that we had died in the land of Egypt! or would God we had died in this wilderness! And wherefore hath the Lord brought us unto this land, to fall by the sword, that our wives and our children should be a prey? were it not better for us to return into Egypt?* (Numbers 14:2-3 KJV)

You probably know some glass-half-full types who live this way. I know that I have known my share. No matter how well their lives are going, they always have a laundry list of complaints waiting to be unfurled. They speak continually, but their words demoralize. They are a murmuring people, not a prophetic people.

The prophetic generation speaks selectively. When the majority squalls, "It's impossible! They'll kill us all! Let's go back to Egypt and enjoy leeks and garlic again," the prophetic generation says, "No thanks. I'd rather eat manna for the rest of my life than miss what God is doing right here."

Murmuring is dangerous. It produces fear and paralyzes the murmurer and his or her listeners. It robbed a generation of Israelites from entering the Promised Land. Think of the seriousness of the consequences: millions of people who were delivered from slavery and released by God into power and prosperity missed the reward of their journey—*because they were afraid.*

Murmuring is also poisonous. When it enters the camp, strife, discontentment, bitterness, and criticism inevitably spread like wildfire. Praise ceases and division reigns. Murmuring is a death sentence to destiny for individuals, nations, and the Church.

A TWIST ON MURMURING

The Hebrew word *luwn* is translated "murmur(ed)" in Numbers 14. It means to "grumble, complain, murmur."[2] It is interesting that the same word is translated elsewhere as "tarry all night," "lodge," and "remain" (see Gen. 19:2; Num. 22:8; Exod. 23:18).[3] Murmuring keeps people mired in the past and extinguishes their destinies.

They Are Visionary

Prophetic people have a big-picture perspective of life. Instead of pining for the leeks and garlic of Egypt, they look forward to the bigger and better harvests—their own harvests—in

Canaan. They do not live in denial of the giants in the land; they are simply not intimidated by them. They know what God has told them and they are willing to contend for what is theirs.

Visionaries have a balanced view of their circumstances and of God's way of unfolding their destinies. They appreciate manna from heaven, but they have no intention of living on it forever. Although they have seen miracles time and time again, they believe the best is yet to come. Always aware of the lessons they have learned, God's prophetic people are confident of becoming more competent with each passing day. Because of their experiences, they realize that they have more to give than they had before.

Prophetic people do not live their lives in the rearview mirror.

They Are Determined to Possess

The prophetic generation is not looking to maintain, but to increase. They are not plateau-dwellers or people who feel that they have arrived. Because they are forward-looking and know who they are, they are determined to make good on their claim and possess the next piece of God-ordained territory.

Anyone can maintain, but only a prophetic people can possess and produce increase. They are alert to God's transitions and become spiritually restless when they have lingered too long. Even when the enemy attempts to constrain them through distractions such as lack, they do not retreat. Instead, they seek God's heart for the way forward. They trust Him to liberate needed resources so they can in turn create a flow of resources to others.

Prophetic people never settle for the status quo. Joshua and Caleb were unwilling to compromise. They refused the complacency of the ten spies and stuck with God's promise.

They knew what He had in mind, and they would only be satisfied by possessing *all of it.*

They Are Servants, Sons, and Daughters

God's prophetic generation values their connection to something bigger than themselves. They do not seek (what the world sees as) their place at the top. They seek first and foremost to be sons and daughters who serve. They honor those who have gone before them and they understand that their predecessors have paved the way and paid the price.

This was certainly true of Elisha. He valued his connection to Elijah and was committed to serving him. When Elijah knew his time on earth was ending, he spoke to his devoted protégé and offered him an easy option. Notice Elisha's response:

> *Then Elijah said to Elisha, "Stay here, please, for the Lord has sent me on to Bethel."*
>
> *But Elisha said, "As the Lord lives, and as your soul lives, I will not leave you!" So they went down to Bethel* (2 Kings 2:2).

The sons of the prophets were a prophetic people who perceived Elijah's imminent departure and prodded Elisha about it:

> *Now the sons of the prophets who were at Bethel came out to Elisha, and said to him, "Do you know that the Lord will take away your master from over you today?"*
>
> *And he said, "Yes, I know; keep silent!"*
>
> *Then Elijah said to him, "Elisha, stay here, please, for the Lord has sent me on to Jericho."*

> *But he said, "As the Lord lives, and as your soul lives, I will not leave you!" So they came to Jericho.*
>
> *Now the sons of the prophets who were at Jericho came to Elisha and said to him, "Do you know that the Lord will take away your master from over you today?"*
>
> *So he answered, "Yes, I know; keep silent!"* (2 Kings 2:3-5)

Elisha silenced the men's questions. His emotions were no doubt surging, yet he remained fixed on his mission—to fulfill and honor his commitment to Elijah, and to realize his own destiny.

Elisha had not been jockeying for the number one position, nor was he distracted by the challenges he knew awaited him. He was only focused on what God was doing in the *now.* He revealed his spiritual maturity by maintaining a sound balance of character and readiness. He was not consumed by concerns with his own ministry or anointing, or worried about whether his lines of supply were about to dry up. All he wanted was to see the transition unfold according to God's plan.

Prophetic people value their spiritual parents. They are open to correction and willing to watch and learn from others. They realize the anointing is caught more than it is taught. They know they are watching and tasting that for which others have paid the price. They honor the fact that their spiritual fathers and mothers have dug deep wells from which they can drink.

That explains Elisha's reaction to the catching up of Elijah: *"Elisha saw it, and he cried out, '**My father, my father,** the* *chariot of Israel and its horsemen!' So he saw him no more. And he took hold of his own clothes and tore them into two pieces"* (2 Kings 2:12).

When Elisha cried, *"My father, my father,"* he acknowledged the enormous chasm created by Elijah's departure. He knew Elijah had kept him centered and balanced. He also knew that the genesis of his kingdom destiny was woven into the relationship the two men shared.

Now his master was gone.

Today's generation is not instinctively Elisha-minded. Many chafe at authority and see servanthood as degrading. Yet, even in the twenty-first century, a prophetic people must have spiritual parents who will set the moral tone, speak the truth regardless of their protégés' success, and bring correction whenever and wherever it is needed.

They Know How to Abide

When Elijah told Elisha to stay behind, he refused. *"But Elisha said, 'As the Lord lives, and as your soul lives,* ***I will not leave you!'*** *So they went down to Bethel"* (2 Kings 2:2). Not once, but four times Elisha refused to leave his master. He knew where he was supposed to be and with whom. How rare this approach is today! In our drive-thru, microwave, no-fault society, staying put through thick and thin is the exception rather than the rule.

Enduring difficulty and sacrifice for the sake of something bigger than us is not a modern mindset. Faithfulness is routinely sacrificed on the altars of convenience and comfort. Instead of being a culture based on principles, we are feelings-driven and prone to fleeing at the first sign of trouble. We recoil when concerned friends get in our "business." We withdraw from church when the pastor says something we don't like hearing. We stop giving when we don't see the "rewards" we hoped to see.

The reality is that we fail to abide when we disconnect from God's eternal purpose. The DNA of a prophetic people causes them to resist this worldly trend. They are motivated by God's proceeding word. They perceive His leading and choose to be at the right place at the right time. Instead of clinging to convenience, they cling to the promise. They are willing to drive 50 miles to be in the right church. They do not balk when God is moving and the service runs long. Prophetic people are determined to abide—not just anywhere or with anyone, but wherever and with whomever God chooses.

They Know How to Receive

Prophetic people know how to persevere *and* how to receive. Whether they drive 50 miles or walk five blocks to get to church, they make sure they are alert when they arrive. God's prophetic people tune in to whatever He is doing or saying at any given moment.

Elisha never took his eyes off Elijah. As the chariot of fire and his master disappeared from view, Elisha continued looking up. Because he was attentive, he saw Elijah's mantle fall from the sky. He knew God was orchestrating the scene, so he did not hesitate to take up the mantle. He knew where it was and he knew it was his.

Elisha valued his time with Elijah, but he also valued the season that would follow. So often we are thrown off by shifting circumstances. We fail to notice that God has sent something of value our way, or we fail to realize that He sent it *for us*.

We wonder, "What is this for?" instead of saying, "Thank You, Lord. I know this is from Your hand. I receive it with gratitude."

Elisha appreciated the mantle that was thrown to him and knew that his job at that moment was simply to pick it up. God would lead him through the rest.

They Know How to Emulate

When Elijah was taken up, Elisha was right where he had left him, but only physically speaking. In every other way, Elisha was in brand new territory. Elijah was gone. The mantle and all that went with it were now Elisha's. Yet he did not see the shift as an opportunity to come out from under his mentor's tutelage. He did not think, "Thank goodness he's gone! Now I can run this ministry my way."

No. Elisha continued to walk in his spiritual father's footsteps. He took the mantle and emulated what Elijah had done before the two men crossed the Jordan (see 2 Kings 2:8). Elisha's first action apart from his master was to copy him:

> *Then* [Elisha] *took the mantle of Elijah that had fallen from him, and struck the water, and said, "Where is the Lord God of Elijah?" And when he also had struck the water, it was divided this way and that; and Elisha crossed over* (2 Kings 2:14).

We Americans tend to be preoccupied with "being ourselves." We value our individuality (as we should), but we are prone to elevating its importance above God's priorities. This happens too often in ministries—those who are new to the ministry are so concerned with being their own people in the Spirit that they overlook the importance of learning from others.

When I first got into the ministry, I did not start out by reinventing the wheel. I'd seen my father cast out demons and I knew his way worked. When I came face to face with my first case of demonic oppression, I followed Dad's example. I looked at the poor woman frothing at the mouth and growling like a dog, and I addressed her tormentor, saying, "You foul spirit from the pit of hell, I command you to come out!" I was not looking to showboat or prove my originality. I emulated my father, and you know what? That demon took off.

Prophetic people are not too proud to emulate those who have gone before them. They are satisfied to start with what they know, and they are willing to allow God to develop their individual ministry styles in His timing.

They Become Elevated

The sons of the prophets revered Elijah, but when they saw Elisha's first prophetic act with Elijah's mantle, they recognized the spiritual transaction that had occurred:

> *Now when the sons of the prophets who were from Jericho saw him, they said,* ***"The spirit of Elijah rests on Elisha."*** *And they came to meet him, and bowed to the ground before him* (2 Kings 2:15).

The men acknowledged Elisha's "promotion" and honored him. They said, in essence, "We're here to serve you, just as we served Elijah."

The sons of the prophets also understood that Elisha's choices made him eligible to succeed Elijah. Prophetic people keep their eyes on God and their hearts fixed on His plan. As a result, they are promoted—not because they seek to be elevated, but because they are stepping into their destinies.

Elisha walked in the activation of all God had in mind for his life. He had just suffered the loss of his beloved spiritual father, yet he remained even-keeled, aware of his surroundings and of what God desired to do next. When the leaders of Jericho told him about the city's poor water and unproductive land, he did not miss a beat. He instructed them and brought forth a word from God:

> *And he said, "Bring me a new bowl, and put salt in it." So they brought it to him. Then he went out to the source of the water, and cast in the salt there, and said, "Thus says the Lord: 'I have healed this water; from it there shall be no more death or barrenness'"* (2 Kings 2:20-21).

Verse 22 goes on to say that the waters and the land were healed as Elisha commanded. He clearly walked under the power of his prophetic mantle, just as Elijah had before him.

The profile of a prophetic people is a profile of God's anointing and power. It is not meant to describe a select few, either people or churches. The day is coming when it will describe the entirety of His glorious universal Church!

This is the Church I and others are fighting for: a generation of people—young and old and from every background—who will be so saturated in the power and anointing of God that they will revolutionize the world. This will not be a people satisfied to tell their grandchildren about what Smith Wigglesworth or Aimee Semple McPherson did back in the day. They will talk about the great exploits *they* did in God's name. They will pass the mantle of burden-removing, yoke-destroying power to the next generation, so that the anointing is never on the decrease, but always on the increase.

I see the day coming when true apostles, prophets, evangelists, pastors, and teachers will cover the earth with His proceeding word and transmit their hunger for the power, presence, and anointing of God across every continent. May you and I be part of that day!

Think on This

Which of the profile points discussed seems most familiar for you? Which ones reflect your personal strengths? Your weaknesses? Are you surrounded by prophetic people? Do you have a spiritual father or mother who invests in your growth? Are you mentoring others? Are you hungry—and if not, have you asked God to revive your hunger and thirst for Him?

Notes

1. *Blue Letter Bible,* Dictionary and Word Search for "*dowr*" (Strong's 1755), Blue Letter Bible, 1996–2011, http://www.blueletterbible.org/lang/lexicon/lexicon.cfm?Strongs=H1755&t=KJV (accessed December 2, 2011).
2. *Blue Letter Bible,* Dictionary and Word Search for "*luwn*" (Strong's 3885), Blue Letter Bible, 1996-2011, http:// www.blueletterbible.org/lang/lexicon/lexicon.cfm?Strongs=H3885&t=KJV (accessed December 3, 2011).
3. Ibid.

Chapter 5

Our Prophetic Weaponry

For the weapons of our warfare are not carnal but mighty in God for pulling down strongholds, casting down arguments and every high thing that exalts itself against the knowledge of God, bringing every thought into captivity to the obedience of Christ (2 Corinthians 10:4-5).

Satan is at war with the prophetic Church. And since God is a speaking God, His Church is a speaking Body. When His voice is heard, atmospheres shift, demonic works are reversed, and lives are rescued from Satan's pit.

This war is not new. Centuries ago, prophets were silenced by the sword and other atrocities. Men such as Zechariah and John the Baptist were slaughtered outright (see 2 Chron. 24:20-22; Matt. 14:9-12). *The* Prophet, Jesus, was opposed to the point of His death and beyond. And in some parts of the world, prophets are murdered even today.

But murder is not the only way to silence the prophetic. Satan works by many cunning means to "kill" the prophets:

- When humanistic thought quenches the thirst for God, the prophetic voice is silenced.
- When liberal theology denies the gifts of the Holy Spirit, the prophetic voice is silenced.
- When scandal erodes trust, the prophetic voice is silenced.
- When imposters desensitize the Church to truth, the prophetic voice is silenced.
- When the false gospel of universalism is preached, the prophetic voice is silenced.

Satan knows that where there is no prophetic utterance, rebellion has free reign. But exactly how does rebellion get a foothold?

Proverbs 29:18 says, *"Where there is no vision, the people perish..."* (KJV). The New King James Version reads: *"Where there is no revelation, the people cast off restraint."* The Hebrew word translated "vision" or "revelation" is the word *chazown,* meaning, "vision, oracle, prophecy (divine communication)."[1] It is from the root *chazah* meaning, in part, to "prophesy."[2]

When there is no *chazown*, the future becomes obscure. Our connection to divine purpose dissipates and we devise our own rudders. Once we become unhinged from God's plan, hopelessness and demoralization are inevitable.

The process continues when demoralization becomes rebellion. We see this happening all over the world—anger and violence are erupting in every corner of the globe. Lawlessness is commonplace. Respect for authority is evaporating. This downward spiral causes people to do inappropriate and even insane things. Drug abuse, cold-blooded killings, destruction of private and public property, and other over-the-top behaviors manifest along with materialism, extreme immodesty, and promiscuity.

Satan's Fighting Days Are Numbered

Despite the ferocity of the battle, Satan's schemes will not prevail. God's glorious Church will emerge *because He spoke it* (see Eph. 5:27). His prophetic generation is well armed and will fulfill its assignment: to speak His will into the earth and usher in the return of Jesus Christ.

The outcome *is* certain but the battle is real. As is true in every natural or spiritual war, each skirmish is an opportunity. Territory is at stake, the balance of power is subject to shifts, and spoils await the victor. War is not a game, however. It always exacts a price for those who choose to engage in it. In the end, the outcome is decided by those who marshal their mettle and materiel effectively.

Our prophetic arsenal is more powerful than that of any earthly army, because our weapons are *"mighty in God"* (2 Cor. 10:4). They are not designed to dazzle the masses or enhance our spiritual egos; they are for waging war. We must no longer be like children toying with weapons built for grownups. It is time for us to pay the price of spiritual adulthood so that we can war with power and integrity.

In addition to our weapons of warfare, God has delegated to us divine identity, destiny, and responsibility. He has equipped us to go *mano a mano* with the accuser of the brethren, and He has laid the foundation for us to win. He has provided all the support we will ever need. The question each of us must ask is, "Will I play a part in the victory?"

Full Gospel, Full Power

The Word of God is a fierce weapon and a force that cannot be bound. It is powerful beyond anything we can manufacture or comprehend. Hebrews 4:12-13 describes its might and precision perfectly:

> *For the word of God is living and powerful, and sharper than any two-edged sword, piercing even to the division of soul and spirit, and of joints and marrow, and is a discerner of the thoughts and intents of the heart. And there is no creature hidden from His sight, but all things are naked and open to the eyes of Him to whom we must give account.*

The Word is always effective and trustworthy. The questions we must ask involve our interaction with God's Word: Are we open to its transforming power? Do we embrace the whole counsel of God? Have we drawn human boundaries around Scripture?

These are not rhetorical questions. Our response to God's Word determines the benefits we will receive from it. So does our working concept of what His Word is. A diluted, sense-based, or user-friendly "gospel" cannot meet our needs. When the battle is raging, those clinging to Gospel "scraps" will find themselves spiritually disarmed, individually and as congregations.

God's Word will not bow to our biases. If we long for the fruit of its power, we will have to embrace the Word on its terms. I cannot imagine doing otherwise. His proceeding word lifts us above the fray of the battle and reminds us that we are His. It forms a firewall around us and helps us to navigate our wilderness experiences.

Even at the height of His wilderness experience, when He was physically weakened by fasting, Jesus was well armed. When the enemy challenged His diety, His mission, and His commitment to truth, Jesus opened His mouth and said, "It is written" (see Matt. 4:4,7,10).

Mature warriors know how to use their weapons. They do not have a promise-box approach to spiritual warfare. They use all of the assets at their disposal, and refuse to deny any aspect of His power. Seasoned soldiers are serious about the battle because they understand the value of what they are fighting for. They enter combat with *all* of their weapons at the ready.

The Identity Weapon

In Chapter 3, we saw the impact on Peter's life of the three great revelations: divinity, identity, and destiny. Peter faced many daunting situations in the days following His revelation of Jesus as the Christ (see Matt. 16:16). But armed with a clear sense of his divine DNA, Peter was able to rise above the obstacles he faced and withstand every demonic and natural attack. The formerly impulsive, up-and-down disciple prevailed in a hostile environment and finished his course.

Remember that the revelation of identity allows the realization of destiny. When you know who you are, your position is clear, and destiny becomes more than an ethereal dream about "someday." Instead, destiny and purpose become tightly intertwined, causing motivation to increase. Knowing who you are empowers you to take your place without apology or excuse.

Do you see why identity is such a powerful weapon in your arsenal? Instead of wondering and wandering, identity empowers you to stand toe to toe with Satan and say, "Regardless of your schemes, I will not bend. I will not buckle. I may not have a dime to my name or a place to lay my head, but God is who He says He is, and I am who God says I am. I will not relinquish my identity; therefore, devil, you have no choice but to surrender!"

If you understand Jesus's divinity and your identity in Him, you will never be defenseless. This is why I continue to proclaim from the pulpit: *You are who God says you are.* There is nothing cute or coddling about the statement. If you wonder who you are, it is impossible to own or defend your destiny—and I assure you, the enemy will challenge you *daily.* Whether you work for the schools, own your own company, or drive a bus, you are called by God to leave His mark. The enemy will not stand by and watch. His plan is to keep *his* imprint on the earth, and you are a threat to his plan. Your job is to hold onto your identity and the prophetic promises over your life to such a degree that you *cannot* be stopped.

When the devil offered Jesus the kingdoms of the world, Jesus stood His ground (see Matt. 4:8-10). Jesus knew who He was and refused to relinquish His identity. He did not need to prove Himself to anyone, least of all the devil. He simply answered Satan with truth and thwarted his onslaught. By standing firm in who He was (and is), Jesus ensured the fulfillment of His mission.

We need to do the same. When the deceiver tries to strip away our identity—whether through intimidation, shame, or condemnation—we must draw on the knowledge of Jesus's divinity and our *God said* and defend it. Remember that prophetic people never surrender their spiritual identities.[3] To do so is to seal their defeat.

One of the quickest ways to lay down the sword of your identity is to see the promises spoken over your life as being invalid or imaginary. For example, if God calls you to lead worship but your church has no openings, do not assume that your *God said* is inaccurate. Likewise, if you apply for the position and are turned down, do not assume that your *God said* was in your head.

Another trap is to believe that you have been disqualified because of failures or shortcomings. The condemnation trick is precisely what Satan used on Peter after he denied Jesus three times. Be alert to this deception! If the enemy can coax you into handing over your identity weapon, he will cut you to pieces with it—and convince you to relinquish your destiny in the process.

My dad had a strong revelation of these truths. All his life, he preached the goodness of El Shaddai—even during a difficult season when he was broke! Not one to quit on God's promises, he continued to write out his tithe checks and to declare the promise of Malachi 3:10:

> *"Bring all the tithes into the storehouse, that there may be food in My house, and try Me now in this," says the Lord of hosts, "if I will not* ***open for you the windows of heaven and pour out for you such blessing that there will not be room enough to receive it."***

Dad had the three revelations settled in his heart. He never distrusted what God said or doubted his call. Therefore, he saw his *God saids* fulfilled in his life and in the lives of those he pastored.

Armed With Logos and Rhema

We know that our weapons are not carnal, physical weapons, but mighty God-given ones (see 2 Cor. 10). In his letter to the Ephesians, Paul stressed the spiritual nature of the battle and described the weapons of our warfare:

> *For we do not wrestle against flesh and blood, but against principalities, against powers, against the rulers of the darkness of this age, against spiritual hosts of wickedness in the heavenly places. Therefore take up the whole armor of God, that you may be able to withstand in the evil day, and having done all, to stand.*
>
> *Stand therefore, having girded your waist with* ***truth,*** *having put on* ***the breastplate of righteousness,*** *and having shod your feet with* ***the preparation of the gospel of peace;*** *above all, taking* ***the shield of faith*** *with which you will*

> *be able to quench all the fiery darts of the wicked one. And take* ***the helmet of salvation,*** *and* ***the sword of the Spirit,*** *which is the word of God* (Ephesians 6:12-17).

Many comprehensive teachings are available on the subject of spiritual armor. We will briefly discuss two pieces here: the *truth* that girds the warrior's waist and the *sword of the Spirit.* Paul described these pieces and the entire armor in terms of the Roman soldiers' gear.

The Belt of Truth: Logos

The belt circling the Roman warrior's waist anchored the rest of his armor. Although it covered only a small portion of the soldier's body, he was entirely compromised when the belt was missing or damaged.

The belt of *truth* Paul described is the written Word of God, known in the Greek as the *logos.* Paul compares Scripture to the soldier's belt because it is the unifying element of our lives. Its principles hold together the rest of our armor (the shield of faith, the breastplate or righteousness, the helmet of salvation, etc.). They are all-encompassing and therefore enable us to live and war effectively.

The Sword of the Spirit: Rhema

The *"sword of the Spirit"* (Eph. 6:17) also refers to the word of God. In this case, however, Paul was specific in choosing the Greek word *rhema*, which we discussed in Chapter 1. Here is some of what we learned:

> Ephesians 6:17 specifically refers in the Greek to the *rhema* word of God. One definition of *rhema*

> is "that which is or has been uttered by the living voice."[4]
>
> A rhema word is your *God said.* It is more than a word from the Bible (i.e., the *logos,* or written Word of God). A rhema word is a spiritual activator. ... When you receive a rhema word, it speaks directly and specifically *to you.*

Logos becomes rhema when it resonates in a deeply personal way. Have you ever experienced a passage of Scripture "jumping off the page" and into your heart? That's rhema. It is a powerful weapon—a personal, prophetic declaration that can be used to defeat the enemy in the heat of battle. Rhema will cause you to defend your destiny to the hilt. If you continue to stand on it, it will overwhelm demonic threats, silence Satan's voice, and clear your path of every obstacle.

Some time ago, I taught on the biblical keys to conquering depression. During my sermon, I shared Psalm 143:7: *"Answer me speedily, O Lord; my spirit fails! Do not hide Your face from me, lest I be like those who go down into the pit."* In the instant that I shared the verse, it became rhema to me. Immediately, the Lord addressed two stubborn challenges I was facing. It was as though He interrupted my preaching to say, "I can answer you quickly in these things *if you will believe Me to do it."*

His Word altered my perceptions. As far as my natural mind could tell, the two issues would take months or even years to iron out. But when the logos of the 7th verse of Psalm 143 became rhema, everything changed. My wife, Gayla, and I witnessed two interventions that can only be described as miraculous. In one week's time, God answered our prayers—and speedily.

Rhema is a powerful weapon of warfare. With it, I could see the enemy's defeat. I said, "Devil, you are a liar. Everything you've been trying to do to hinder the work of God is now finished. The kingdom work He has given us will go forward *now.*"

Please don't misunderstand me—I am not preaching a doctrine of speedy answers. What I am saying is that when God's Word becomes rhema to you, it is an offensive weapon against which Satan has absolutely no power. Your rhema cannot be revoked or discredited by any person or demon spirit.

Your rhema is from God and it will stand.

Spiritual Gift Cache

Make no mistake: the enemy is out to kill, steal, and destroy (see John 10:10). He goes after your relationships, your work, and your stuff, but he attacks all of that to get to *you.* His goal is simple: to obscure the purposes of God and prevent the fulfillment of your call.

As monumental as your salvation is in eternal terms, the Father has other, more immediate plans for you. He wants to touch the world through you. God has placed inside of you something (or many things) He wishes to use to help others. If you are His born-again child, you are equipped to move in His power to make an eternal difference now, in this life.

Each of us has at least one specific God-given gift. Some are gifted in mercy. They know how to come alongside others and help them walk through troubled times. Others are exhorters—they can barely open their mouths without exuding thermal currents of encouragement that cause other people to soar.

Some gifts seem more practical, but are equally spiritual. Organizers know how to make things work. They arrange systems, spaces, people, and functions for improved productivity and effectiveness. They fine-tune operations so that every drop of effort, expense, and time yields its maximum output. Just as organizers streamline operations, servers are the ones eager to jump in and get the work done. Without them, the vision could not be realized.

These gifts, and many more, are present throughout the Body of Christ and manifest differently in each person and situation. From a "religious" mindset, they seem less significant than the fivefold ministry offices. But they are not. All of the giftings work together; none of them can function alone. In a mature body, everyone recognizes and contributes their gifts. The result is a transformed Church—and a changed world.

There is a level of gifting inherent in your spiritual DNA. You may be called to full-time ministry or some other vocation. But even if you are not called to be the next "Oral Roberts," you can visit the sick and anoint them with oil. And even if God has not called you as a prophet to the nations, He still desires to put His words in your mouth. Whatever your gift may be, recognize it as the valuable and powerful prophetic weapon God intended. And use it!

Roadway Warriors

As you already know, God's speaking is not only predictive but also creative. When He said, *"Let there be light"* (Gen. 1:3), He did more than announce coming attractions. God's words *created* the very light He prophesied. In speaking, God made way for the darkness to be vanquished.

When God speaks to your future, He is doing more than notifying you of what He has in mind. He is creating, in the spirit realm, a literal roadway leading to the destination He describes. That destination is your destiny, and His roadway is the precise and perfect path to take you there. It is not just a mode of travel; it is a stream of resources stocked with everything you need to fulfill His plan.

Your destiny is not a divine version of Pin the Tail on the Donkey. God does not plot your destination only to blindfold you, spin you around, and watch you stumble awkwardly toward it. He sends you on a journey fully outfitted by Him to bring transformation. If you are called to start a business, He is your venture capitalist. If you obey His voice, He will lead you step by step to the resources He ordained at the outset.

Consider the transforming power of God's proceeding word in the lives of our Bible heroes. When Abraham was 75 and childless, God said, *"I will make you a great nation"* (Gen. 12:2). A great nation? From what? A barren couple whose advanced age only made their infertility more impossible to overcome?

Yes! A great nation from the loins of the aged and infertile was exactly what God had in mind. And He delivered. His words transformed barrenness into unimaginable fruitfulness that continues to this day.

Perhaps Abraham and Sarah's testimony encouraged their great-grandson Joseph to hang onto his "impossible" *God said.* Years after his betrayal and imprisonment, Joseph still remembered two dreams that revealed his future. These dreams plowed the path to his promotion by Pharaoh, even before Joseph's brothers sold him to slave traders (see Gen. 37).

The prophetic is not a spiritual fortune cookie or the "light side" of Satan's dark gifts. Nor is the prophetic designed purely to take your mind off your present troubles. The prophetic serves as a bulldozer in the spirit realm. It plows through trees, rocks, structures, mountains, and any other obstacle to carve the perfect roadway to your destiny.

The roadway plowed by the prophetic is spiritual and practical. You wouldn't dream of driving your shiny sedan through thick woods or swampland. Nor would you take your family cross-country on a freeway that was under construction. When you plan a trip, you select a drivable route on roads that have been prepared *ahead of time.*

Your prophetic roadway is marked with signposts that reveal God's timing. If you are mindful of His timing, the road will rise to meet you, so to speak. But if you get ahead of His plan, you will find your road inadequately developed to meet your needs. You will hit unnecessary glitches and setbacks. You might even find yourself lacking provision at key moments and wondering why God has not come through for you. If you have acted in your timing and not His, you will reach what looks like your destination, but it will be unfinished and unprepared to sustain you.

If you have ever jumped the gun, you know how costly your impatience can be. This can happen if your view of the prophetic is incomplete. For example, if you see it (even unwittingly) as God's version of psychic power, you will focus on His predictive intent and not the creative work that is part of His prophetic operation. In other words, you will concentrate on the destination but be unconcerned about the prophetic roadway He is preparing to take you there. The journey will be all about arriving, and not about waiting for Him.

That is a setup for failure. Scripture says that *"those who wait on the Lord shall renew their strength; they shall mount up with wings like eagles, they shall run and not be weary, they shall walk and not faint"* (Isa. 40:31). Conversely, those who do not wait on the Lord are weakened by their follies. In trying to make things work, they grow weary, become demoralized, and often give up.

War Is Messy

If you are planning to reach your destination, you must realize what is ahead. There will be skirmishes and setbacks. Some of the battles you face will be the work of the enemy. Some will result from your unwillingness to obey God or to change.

Either way, war is messy. My choice of words is not meant to trivialize the experiences of those who have witnessed the horrors of flesh and blood war. What I am talking about here is spiritual warfare. Although it does not directly involve the spilling of human blood, it has eternal consequences. And it is being waged in the heavenlies right now.

For much of the Church, warfare is ignored or even denied. Without realizing they are in the fight, believers suffer casualties and live far below the level of blessing and purpose that God intends for them. Until the whole Church recognizes the reality of the spiritual battlefield, Christians will continue to take incoming fire, and many will blame God for the losses suffered.

Every one of us wants God's promises to be manifested in our lives. However, most of us want them to fall into place without a fight, as the ten spies did in Numbers 13 and 14. We dislike it when progress disturbs the status quo we have worked so hard to cultivate. When our lives are neat and tidy, we feel secure and in control. We want God to move within the parameters we find comfortable. We naively or stubbornly ask Him to transform our lives without messing with our perspectives and routines.

If we are honest, real life is messy and warfare is part of it. The Scriptures assure us that we are at war. Why else would Paul tell us to *"take up the whole armor of God"* (Eph. 6:13)? And why would he have reminded Timothy to *"war a good warfare"* (1 Tim. 1:18 KJV)?

Without warfare, we cannot experience victory or the growth we desire. Almost without exception, we must *undergo* something in order to *overcome.* The good news is that we never undergo anything alone. God is with us and has equipped us with His mighty arsenal, including a *God said.*

Over the years, my *God said* has driven me to do some messy-looking things. I have believed for victory when defeat was all anyone could see. I have prophesied to empty pews, not because a full church will stroke my ego, but because He has promised revival in my region. If talking to inanimate objects is my part of His plan, so be it. It might not be the polished picture people see when I am in the pulpit. The folks who are used to seeing me in shined shoes and a sharp suit might never see me talking to the pews in a long night of intercession. They may never know that I prayed them and their kids into those pews.

God did not build our sanctuary and bring our congregation into being in a day. Our influence in the region and the world did not develop overnight. Nor was I a bystander in the process. I had to take up my weapons and fight the good fight. When it looked like my *God said* was impossible, I had to see past the impossibility. In order to see my *God said* activated, I had to remember it, day in and day out.

War *is* messy. If you have a dream of any magnitude at all, you have to fight the good fight, and you have to do it when dry bones surround you. Only you can walk the roadway God has plowed to your destiny. If you will do it, He will see that you arrive right on time. It won't be pretty every step of the way, but it will be worth it.

More often than not, you must undergo to overcome.

Anti-Status-Quo Munitions

Nobody knows more about dry bones than the prophet Ezekiel. The status quo confronting him was dismal. Any sense of comfort was lost. There was no telling how long Judah's dark season would last, and still the people were stiff-necked. Ezekiel warned them of God's judgment, and was among the exiles taken to Babylon when Jerusalem fell. The worst-case scenario had become reality. And still, God gave Ezekiel a message of restoration.

God took the prophet, in a vision, to a valley littered with dry bones (see Ezek. 37). The picture of Israel's scattered people and decimated nation could not be clearer. Yet in the midst of it, God offered hope. Much as Jesus did with Peter, God gave

Ezekiel a revelation after first asking a tough question: *"Son of man, can these bones live?"* (Ezek. 37:3).

Ezekiel had no clue what the right answer was, and freely admitted it:

> [He] *answered, "O Lord God, You know."*
>
> *Again He said to me, "Prophesy to these bones, and say to them, 'O dry bones, hear the word of the Lord! Thus says the Lord God to these bones: "Surely I will cause breath to enter into you, and you shall live. I will put sinews on you and bring flesh upon you, cover you with skin and put breath in you; and you shall live. Then you shall know that I am the Lord"'"* (Ezekiel 37:3-6).

God commanded the prophet to attack the status quo by speaking to the bones. This was a clue to His intended outcome, as was His next statement: *"Then you shall know that I am the Lord."* Ezekiel did not ask any questions; he simply obeyed God's instruction and spoke to the bones. When he did...

> *...there was a noise, and suddenly a rattling; and the bones came together, bone to bone. Indeed, as I looked, the sinews and the flesh came upon them, and the skin covered them over; but there was no breath in them*
>
> *Also He said to me, "Prophesy to the breath, prophesy, son of man, and say to the breath, 'Thus says the Lord God: "Come from the four winds, O breath, and breathe on these slain, that they*

> *may live.'"" So I prophesied as He commanded me, and breath came into them, and they lived, and stood upon their feet, an exceedingly great army* (Ezekiel 37:7-10).

Ezekiel commanded the bones to obey the word of the Lord. It was a creative act by which the breath returned, tissues were created, and the dry bones reattached and became whole again. On its face, the scene was bizarre. To the average bystander, Ezekiel would have seemed insane. (I am sure that many people would question my prophesying to the pews too!) But it does not matter how crazy our obedience looks. What matters is that His will is done and His creative power is released in a dead and dying world!

What matters is that the status quo—the "go along to get along" mindset—is uprooted and the holy intent of the Most High God is made manifest in the plain sight of saints and sinners alike. You and I have been assigned to use our God-ordained weapons—all of our weapons—to accomplish our mission in the earth. It is time to plow new roadways. It is time to ascend to places in Him that we have never seen. It is time for the Church to be the Church.

Think on This

How do you react to the topic of warfare? Were you already aware of the weapons God has given you? Are you more aware of them now? How do you feel about that? Do you see yourself as an empowered or reluctant warrior? Explain. What questions does this chapter raise for you? Will you take them to prayer or put them on the shelf. Why?

Notes

1. *Blue Letter Bible,* Dictionary and Word Search for *"chazown"* (Strong's 2377), Blue Letter Bible, 1996-2011, http://www.blueletterbible.org/lang/lexicon/lexicon.cfm?Strongs=H2377&t=KJV (accessed December 8, 2011).
2. Biblesoft's *New Exhaustive Strong's Numbers and Concordance with Expanded Greek-Hebrew Dictionary.* CD-ROM. Biblesoft, Inc. and International Bible Translators, Inc. (© 1994, 2003, 2006) s.v. "chazah," (OT 2372).
3. For more on this, see Chapter 4: Profile of a Prophetic People.
4. *Blue Letter Bible,* Dictionary and Word Search for *"rhēma"* (Strong's 4487), Blue Letter Bible, 1996–2011, http://www.blueletterbible.org/lang/lexicon/lexicon.cfm?Strongs=G4487&t=KJV (accessed November 17, 2011).

Chapter 6

The Prophetic Anointing and Response

Be sure to use the abilities God has given you through His prophets when the elders of the church laid their hands upon your head. Put these abilities to work; throw yourself into your tasks so that everyone may notice your improvement and progress. Keep a close watch on all you do and think. Stay true to what is right and God will bless you and use you to help others (1 Timothy 4:14-16 TLB).

The Church is at a crossroads. In many sectors, Christianity has been neutralized. Sanctuaries and sermons are devoid of the cross, the blood, and the anointing. Secularization and CEO-style leaders have created social-club atmospheres in which truth is less important than emotion, transformation gives way to accommodation, and attendance outranks the authentic move of the Holy Spirit.

This bodes poorly for the future. A generational transaction must occur for the Church to continue as Christ's active Body in the earth. We cannot take the anointing of God to the grave with us; we *must* transfer it to the next generation. If we fail, the power of God will be nothing more than a memory in three or four generations.

These are strong statements, and rightly so. Much of the American Church has lost sight of the Holy Spirit. We suck down motivational messages that mask our deeper spiritual needs. We are willing to compromise the integrity of the anointing in order to appeal to everyone and offend no one. An increasingly diluted "gospel" expedites secular drift and euthanizes morality.

Yet the extinction of the anointing can be averted. The Church must desire more than fiscal viability and passive influence in the community. If we will preach the true Gospel, reach beyond our walls *in His power*, and take our respective positions in the Body and the culture, a new wave of anointing will revive our planet.

It will not happen by accident. We must value the anointing and the price paid for it by our forbears. Future generations must know the power of God firsthand. When they do, they will worship Him without reservation and they will pay the price for future generations to know Him.

Gifts and Anointing

The authentic spiritual gifts and the unction of the Holy Spirit are at the core of the prophetic Church. Their importance as revealed in Scripture is indisputable. We have touched on these subjects in other chapters. Here Paul explains the source and nature of spiritual giftings and the purpose of the anointing:

> *There are diversities of gifts, but the same Spirit. There are differences of ministries, but the same Lord. And there are diversities of activities, but it is the same God who works all in all. But the manifestation of the Spirit is given to each one for the profit of all* (1 Corinthians 12:4-7).

In a brief paragraph, Paul states three foundational points: there are many types of spiritual gifts; all gifts originate with God; the anointing, or manifestation of the Spirit, is designed to benefit everyone. His letter continues by naming individual gifts: the word of wisdom, word of knowledge, gift of faith, gifts of healing, working of miracles, prophecy, discerning of spirits, tongues, and the interpretation of tongues (see 1 Cor. 12:8-10). Paul reiterates the source of spiritual gifts and their diversity by saying, *"But one and the same Spirit works all these things, distributing to each one individually as He wills"* (1 Cor. 12:11).

Gifts and anointing are God's idea. When the presbytery (the spiritually mature) laid hands on Timothy and prophesied over him, a spiritual transaction occurred (see 1 Tim. 4:14). Paul counseled Timothy to remain mindful of its significance and not neglect the deposit made within him.

Creativity is an essential element of the transaction Paul described, as we have seen. When God speaks, He creates what is to come. When you are regularly bathed in a prophetic atmosphere, and even when you receive a personal prophecy on a given day, giftings are deposited and activated.

Gifts are not chosen by us, but are distributed by the Holy Spirit *"individually as He wills"* (1 Cor. 12:11). These deposits are not based on age, gender, talent, or personal charisma. Nor can gifts be taught to someone in whom God's deposit has not been made. For example, if you are called as an evangelist but I teach you everything I know about operating in the prophetic office, the only thing you will learn is how to "play" a role that "looks like" that of the prophet.

It is not my intent to create a class of spiritual elites. The anointing is intrinsic to the Body of Christ because the Spirit of God dwells within the born-again believer. As we will see in Chapter 8, callings and anointing vary. Whatever your calling may be, however, you are anointed to speak life—on the job, at the dinner table, or on the train. The anointing has no boundaries, so wherever you are, His power goes with you!

You carry His anointing, and yet you are not called to be a container. You are called to be a conduit pouring out what you have received—dreams, visions, revelation, anointing, gifts, and words—to those around you. This happens first to your bloodline and your spiritual sons and daughters, but also to strangers, coworkers, friends, and acquaintances.

Anointing: Purpose and Effects

The anointing is not about spiritual thrills or goose bumps, although a genuine move of God usually produces some form of physical response. The anointing is designed to mature, equip, and complete God's people. Take for example the fivefold ministry gifts. Men and women are called to these offices with the intent that their anointings (apostle, prophet, evangelist, pastor, and teacher) would combine and intersect *"for the equipping of the saints for the work of ministry, for the edifying of the body of Christ"* (Eph. 4:12).

These combined "chemistries" serve to strengthen us individually and corporately. I often hear pastors say that their churches are hospitals for broken people. I understand the intended humility of this statement. None of us has arrived and all of us have been wounded in life. But the glorious Church God has ordained is only possible when we outgrow our need to be spiritually and emotionally propped up.

This is one reason why generational transfer is so important. The Church must build upon its past successes. But so often we fail to do so. We ride revival waves and then ebb into complacency, desperate to be revived again. If we build on revival, however, the long-term results will go "viral"—instead of fizzling out, they will catapult around the globe.

To achieve this model someone has to buck the current trend. We need leaders who resist catering to perceived needs and instead minister to spiritual root issues. My fellow pastors: we cannot be more committed to doing what the people want than we are to doing what God has called us to do. Direction for the house of God does not come from the hemline up; it moves from the head down. We leaders cannot be timid about our spiritual authority. We must not abuse or corrupt it—but we must walk in it.

To engender a prophetic generation, we must get back to the basics: not functioning from philosophies, programs, or personal strengths, but from our dependency on the *dunamis* power of the Holy Spirit. Strong's describes *dunamis* as "force (literally or figuratively); specially, miraculous power (usually by implication, a miracle itself)."[1] Simply stated, it is the limitless ability of God. When *dunamis* is in operation, the works of the devil are destroyed.

This is essential within the church and outside our walls. The plain truth is that the Church is being impacted by the world at least as much as the reverse is happening. If we were to compare morals within today's Church with the world's morals from 50 years ago, those of today's Church would be worse! We might not realize it because we have become desensitized to it, but the slippage is evident. Even simple modesty in women's dress has become passé as young women—and their mothers!—blindly follow Hollywood's lead.

If we are to break the spirit of hell rather than succumb to it, we must exercise our authority and His power over the enemy and his works. We need the *dunamis* of God.

Spirit Direction, Not Human Perception

The anointing is for God's purposes. Therefore, He uses it His way, often by asking us to do things that seem illogical to the natural eye. Years ago, I preached at a historic Pentecostal church in the state of Texas. At some point, God prompted me to minister to a man sitting in the next-to-last row. I sensed the Lord's desire to impart something to the man, but I was unsure what it was or what He wanted me to say. Nevertheless, I called the man out, intending to tell him as much as I knew.

In the milliseconds before I could speak, the Holy Spirit arrested me and said, "Don't say the word *impartation.* Say *transmission.*"

I argued with the Holy Spirit saying, "If I say that, they'll think I'm ignorant." Thank God, I surrendered my argument quickly and said, "Sir, the only thing I have come to tell you is that God is getting ready to give you a transmission of the Holy Spirit."

The wording seemed goofy, but the church exploded in shouting and dancing and praise. There was such a commotion I thought maybe an angel had appeared behind me or Jesus had been seen hovering over us. Uncertain what was up, I proceeded to lay my hands on the man. The power of God hit him and he fell to the floor.

I did not understand what the transmission thing was all about until later, when I learned about the man's nickname: Transmission Man. Everyone knew that he owned several auto transmission shops in town. Had I disregarded God's choice of vocabulary, I would have missed out on effectively ministering in His power. In our learnedness and efforts to be profound, we can be profoundly stupid—and powerless.

Integrity of the Anointing

Protecting the integrity of the anointing involves everyone on both ends of the gifts. We must regard the anointing if we are to benefit from its flow. We must be vigilant, however, to sift out counterfeits. This is not a matter of formality, but urgency. For example, when a word is delivered that is not from God (whether it is demonic or flesh-driven), it still functions as seed. For better or worse, that seed *will* produce fruit.

When instructing the Corinthian church, Paul wrote: *"Let two or three prophets speak, and* ***let the others judge****"* (1 Cor. 14:29).

We know that prophecy plows the road to future fulfillment. Therefore, the judging of prophecy is essential to the proper prophetic response. If improper or inaccurate prophecies are given place, those who come into agreement with them can wander through months, years, and even decades on paths of confusion and error.

Prophecy must be judged whether a prophet delivers it to the nations or to a prophetically-inclined son or daughter of God. Remember that First Corinthians 14:3 requires all prophecy to edify, exhort, and comfort. Prophecy must also be judged in light of Scripture. If a prophet tells you to leave your husband so you can be free to do itinerant ministry, you are hearing from a false prophet!

Prophecy must also bear witness to our spirits. If it stirs confusion, set it aside and wait for the Holy Spirit to bring clarity. And always, recruit a mature believer to listen to the prophecy and judge it. Not long ago, a young man approached me with a word he had received. He asked, "Pastor, would you read this? Do you think it's from God?"

I answered, "Well, I haven't meditated on it or prayed about it, but it is in harmony with Scripture. It seems appropriate and godly and I see no red flags here." I appreciated the young man's willingness to seek counsel. I wish people would do it more.

If only all leaders had the sense of this young fellow! Once, at a church where I was invited as a guest speaker, I experienced the complete breakdown of prophetic order. Things started off great: the crowd was standing room only and God had moved powerfully during the service. But at the end, the pastor invited anyone who had a word to speak.

The pastor's announcement was bizarre in its thoughtlessness. The service quickly degenerated into mayhem as the microphone made the rounds. Then a man prophesied something unforgettable for all the wrong reasons. He declared: "As Gepetto loved Pinocchio, so the Lord loves you."

The next 30 minutes were pure chaos. One man shared a vision and other people proceeded to tell him what the vision meant. Before I knew it, arguments were breaking out over the differences in interpretation. A powerful move of God had deteriorated into a freak show. It happened because of a lapse in leadership, a lack of seriousness regarding the gifts, and the failure to judge prophecy.

It was a mess! Loose cannons were firing all over the sanctuary. The prophetic gifts were trashed; the Holy Spirit was dishonored; and people were no doubt left in confusion. This is the very kind of silliness and abuse that have been, to me, the greatest heartbreak in more than 40 years of ministry.

Passing the Generational Torch

The prophetic anointing must be protected if it is to be passed to the next generation. In God's plan, the anointing does not dissipate; instead, it becomes greater over time. Our spiritual sons and daughters should stand on our shoulders and move in greater dimensions of the Spirit than we have known.

Satan vehemently opposes the upward trend. His strategy is to whittle away at the anointing until it has been cut off. One of his tactics is to interrupt the generational transfer from taking place. If he can convince one generation that their parents' spiritual experiences and personal relationships with Christ are irrelevant, he will achieve his ends. We must prevent this outcome—not by crafting a user-friendly facsimile of relevance, but by exposing the next generation to the sheer power, truth, and love of God. When they experience the anointing firsthand, their need for relevance will be more than met.

Paul's protégé Timothy is a New Testament example of someone to whom the generational torch was passed. He hailed from a strong spiritual bloodline, which Paul described as *"the genuine faith that is in you, which dwelt first in your grandmother Lois and your mother Eunice, and I am persuaded is in you also"* (2 Tim. 1:5). Timothy inherited multigenerational faith.

The people I pastor hear about my father's anointing often. Those who have been with us awhile know about how my dad laid hands on 53 deaf people in Brazil, and they remember that all 106 ears were opened. When I share Dad's testimonies, I realize that I am repeating myself; but I do it for a reason. It is my job to make sure they never forget the greatness of God or the power of a multigenerational anointing. When they see my sons, Adam and Aaron, pastoring and operating in their gifts, I want them to appropriate the promise of spiritual legacy and imprint it upon their families. It is their job to make sure that their children never forget that God heals the sick, delivers the bound, and raises the dead.

We must ensure that there will be Elishas in place when our Elijahs are gone. We have talked about the importance of spiritual fatherhood,[2] and we saw how Elisha valued the seasoned prophet's mentorship. Elisha saw himself as the elder man's servant and son. In so doing, he placed himself in Elijah's spiritual bloodline. He abided in the place of spiritual formation under Elijah's leadership and was positioned to "catch" the anointing (the mantle) of the elder prophet.

EVER-INCREASING FAITH AND POWER

When we pass the anointing to the next generation, we give them something to build upon. We want them to reach greater heights at younger ages. Many in my generation learned to use computers as adults. Now, our kids and grandkids use computers as toddlers, with no hesitation at all.

When I was a child, my father taught me the things he had learned the hard way in his adulthood. I have done the same with my children. They knew things as adolescents that I had not figured out until my 30s. That is the dynamic of generational increase and true prosperity.

LOOK UP AND ALIGN

How we respond to the prophetic eternally impacts us. Always, we must begin by remembering that His ways and thoughts are higher than ours (see Isa. 55:8-9). We must look upward in order to grasp them. As the psalmist wrote: *"I will lift up my eyes to the hills—from whence comes my help? My help comes from the Lord, who made heaven and earth"* (Ps. 121:1-2).

God dwells in a high place. We look "up" to Him by aligning ourselves with His higher thoughts and ways. This is an essential of prophetic response. When we see His plan from His limitless perspective, we are able to get on board with it. This is a key of destiny fulfillment.

This is why it is so important for us to understand how God sees us. He said: *"For I know the plans I have for you... plans to prosper you and not to harm you, plans to give you hope and a future"* (Jer. 29:11 NIV). Religious mindsets train us to question God's concern for us. Therefore, our default setting is to disagree with or distrust the great things He has promised. Until His unending love is settled in our hearts, we will unconsciously oppose His promises and wonder why they fail to manifest.

It is so simple: Our confidence in God is predicated on our impression of who He is and what He thinks. If we are convinced of His good intentions toward us, we receive His promises. When we *know* Him, we are not surprised when He leads us to victory, provides abundantly, or heals our bodies. We know He is Jehovah Nissi (God our Banner), Jehovah Jireh (God our Provider), and Jehovah Rophe (God our Healer).

Our sights must be cast upward! When God called Isaiah, he said: *"I saw the Lord sitting on a throne,* ***high and lifted up,*** *and the train of His robe filled the temple"* (Isa. 6:1). When we see the Lord in this way, we can stand tall in every situation, confident of His ability to handle the problem and conquer every enemy. Divorce, bankruptcy, and illness—*nothing* will be able to strip God's promises from us.

A WORD OUT OF SEASON

The prophetic anointing often produces a word that seems out of season. Imagine in the midst of an economic downturn, God speaking to you about starting a business. Your heart leaps at the prospect, but His words seem like a terrible idea when you consider the economic environment.

Noah received an out-of-season word from God (see Gen. 6). Although rain had never fallen on the earth, God told him to prepare for a massive flood. Imagine how absurd God's instructions must have seemed!

Nevertheless, God provided all the details for building the vessel, and Noah followed them exactly. Can you picture the jeering when his neighbors strained their necks to look up at the massive ark? It was, after all, designed to address a reality for which they had no frame of reference—*yet*.

Has God spoken such a word to you? Are you ready to embrace it?

The Prophetic Response: Fully Persuaded

When your thinking is aligned with God's, you respond to Him in ways that facilitate the fulfillment of His promised blessings. Abraham's response to God's promises is a great example. It demonstrated His trust in God and superseded his belief in human limitations, as Paul explained:

> *Against hope* (Abraham) *believed in hope, that he might become the father of many nations; according to that which was spoken, So shall thy seed be. And being not weak in faith, he considered not his own body now dead, when he was about an hundred years old, neither yet the deadness of Sara's womb: he staggered not at the promise of God through unbelief; but was strong in faith, giving glory to God; and* ***being fully persuaded*** *that, what He had promised, He was able also to perform* (Romans 4:18-21 KJV).

The word *promise* in this passage deals with the idea of prophecy, specifically "an announcement...information, assent or pledge; especially a divine assurance of good..."[3] Everything about Abraham's walk involved God's prophetic promise of his fathering a great nation. The reality of the promise would not become clear until Israel numbered in the millions—as captives in Egypt.

When God promised a great nation from Abraham's loins, the patriarch and his wife had not yet produced a single son. Yet Abraham did not stagger at the promise. This steadfastness was key to its activation. To stagger at the promise would be to call God a liar. How difficult, if not impossible, would it be to believe a liar?

Abraham did not have proof, nor did he request any before taking God's promise to heart. He simply trusted what God said despite his circumstances. We know that God cannot lie. We know that He is omnipotent. Clearly, His efforts cannot fail. How can our prophetic response be less trusting than Abraham's? Abraham had no Bible to back up God's claims. There were no "faith conventions" or DVDs to encourage him in the dark seasons. Yet Abraham was fully persuaded.

When we are fully persuaded of God's promise, it forces us to reach a higher level. The things He says supersede the level of our current ability to operate; therefore, faith is cultivated. Little by little, we learn to function and succeed in a higher realm, a place where newer, greater possibilities become easier to see. Being fully persuaded leads us to more and more faith in Him and better and better results.

THE FATHER THINKS BIG

When we think we are "aiming for the stars," we are still shooting for something less than what God has in mind. Allow me to use a financial analogy, since everyone can relate to money matters:

Suppose your income is in the five-figure range, but your dream is to earn $100,000 in a single year. To you, breaking into six figures is *big,* but to God the idea is less radical. He always sees things higher and bigger. We get stuck when our thinking forbids us from seeing things His way.

Our "small" thinking is based, not on His ability or plan, but on our perceptions and degraded self-image. Without realizing it, we undercut God's promises and deny the entrance of His awesome power in our lives. It's time to swing for the fences!

Anatomy of the Prophetic Response

In Chapter 4, we saw the faithless response of the ten spies contrasted with the warrior spirit of Joshua and Caleb. The latter men were fully persuaded of the promises of God. In their minds, God's promise superseded any threat of giants. The ten spies saw the situation inside out. Having seen the physical evidence of God's promise, they discounted it with a single word: "Nevertheless" (see Num. 13–14).

Remember the context of God's promise: Over the course of centuries, beginning with Abraham, He prophesied the taking of the Promised Land. God reaffirmed His promise to Isaac and Jacob, and even Joseph referred to it. If that were not enough, God reiterated His promise to Moses, who sent the 12 spies to assess the land.[4]

Having heard from God repeatedly and having scouted out the land for themselves, the ten spies said something almost unbelievable:

> *We went to the land where you sent us.* ***It truly flows with milk and honey,*** *and this is its fruit.*

> ***Nevertheless*** *the people who dwell in the land are strong; the cities are fortified and very large; moreover we saw the descendants of Anak* (the giants) *there* (Numbers 13:27-28).

The ten spies confirmed the truth of God's promise and still responded in fear and unbelief! This is not the prophetic response we want to cultivate.

The ten fearful men were plagued with doubt. Instead of being excited, they sulked and whined. They saw the lush fruit (grapes so large it took two men to carry a single bunch), yet they obsessed on the presence of enemies in the land. God had already promised their enemies' defeat; but the ten spies could not see past their own weakness. Instead, they relinquished their identity in God. They discarded what God said (the truth) and believed their own imaginations (the lies); therefore, instead of being joyful, they wallowed in self-pity. They stood on the very threshold of the Promised Land and begged to return to Egypt (see Num. 13:27–14:4).

Joshua and Caleb's behavior was diametrically opposite. Their choices reveal the quintessential prophetic response: words and actions that activate the promise. Consider the contrasts:

1. The ten spies succumbed to doubt. Joshua and Caleb remained fully persuaded. They believed they were *"well able to overcome"* the land (Num. 13:30).

2. The ten spies grumbled. Joshua and Caleb rejoiced over the evidence. They called the land *"exceedingly good"* (Num. 14:7).

3. The ten spies focused on the enemy. Joshua and Caleb focused on the promise. Because God was behind the promise, they trusted in it more than the problem (see Num. 14:8).

4. The ten spies trusted in limited human ability. Joshua and Caleb relied on God's strength. They said, *"the Lord is with us"* (Num. 14:9).

5. The ten spies forgot who they were. Joshua and Caleb never relinquished their identity in God. They did not see themselves as grasshoppers; instead, they saw the giants as their bread (see Num. 14:9).

6. The ten spies embraced a lie. Joshua and Caleb believed the truth. They stuck with God's word to them and cautioned the Israelites not to *"rebel against the Lord"* (Num. 14:9).

7. The ten spies displayed a victim mentality. Joshua and Caleb rejected self-pity and regret. Instead, they pointed out the enemy's disadvantaged position, saying, *"Their protection has departed from them"* (Num. 14:9).

8. The ten spies cursed their situation. Joshua and Caleb saw it as their launch pad. They said boldly, *"Let us go up at once and take possession"* (Num. 13:30).

What a testimony of pure faith, and what an example to follow! You might not be facing literal giants, but there is a territory that God is leading you to take. Because of the finished work of the cross, you are better equipped to take it than even Joshua and Caleb were. So go for it.

THREE POWERFUL RESPONSES

When Elijah approached the widow of Zarephath (whom God appointed to provide for him), she was at the end of her provisions and ready to serve a final meal for her and her son. They would eat one last time before starvation would take them out. Elijah spoke an out-of-season word: he asked her to feed him first and then see God's unending provision. Her response? She baked him a cake. The result? She received the promise (see 1 Kings 17:8-16).

When Naaman, the leprous commander of Syria's army, sought healing, Elisha sent a messenger with instructions for his cleansing: wash in the filthy waters of the Jordan River seven times. Naaman was insulted that Elisha did not come himself; he was also skeptical of the Jordan. Yet, when his servants urged him to follow Elisha's instructions, he did, *"and his flesh was restored like the flesh of a little child, and he was clean"* (2 Kings 5:14; see 5:1-14).

When a recently widowed woman was informed by her husband's debtors that her sons would be enslaved in lieu of payment, she cried out to Elisha. The prophet told her to borrow all the empty vessels she could find and fill them with the little bit of oil she had left. Although Elisha's request seemed illogical, the widow obeyed, and the oil was miraculously multiplied. It was enough to pay her debt and support her family for the rest of their lives (see 2 Kings 4:1-7).

"He who receives you receives Me, and he who receives Me receives Him who sent Me. He who receives a prophet in the name of a prophet shall receive a prophet's reward..." (Matthew 10:40-41).

Prophetic Prosperity and Your Response

The prophetic response activates prophetic fulfillment. In the kingdom, fulfillment produces prophetic prosperity. To enjoy prophetic prosperity, we must embrace the truth of God's love. We must realize that He desires the fulfillment of His promises even more than we do. In fact, He loves surprising us by doing things we have not even asked of Him.

Through King Jehoshaphat, God told His people: *"Believe in the Lord your God, and you shall be established; believe His prophets, and you shall prosper"* (2 Chron. 20:20). I don't have to be a prophet to tell you that life is about choices. You can believe and receive the things of God or you can be cynical and reject them.

You must decide whether you will choose the ways of the ten spies or the ways of Joshua and Caleb. Put yourself in the Bible accounts you have read and ask yourself whether you would respond as the widow of Zarephath, Naaman, and the indebted widow did. Determine where you really stand: Do you want to see God's prophetic promises fulfilled in your life, or are you satisfied to live out your days at your current level of fulfillment?

It's time to take inventory. How badly do you want the promise? How much of the promise do you want? If you want it all, then revisit the evidence He has given you so far. Rejoice in the vision and remember that He has positioned you for fulfillment. There may be obstacles in your path; there may be squatters on the land; you may have questions in your mind that are as yet unanswered; the promise might even seem impossible—but God is able and He is with you. Even your enemies have been offered as your bread.

Honestly examine your approach to God's move in your life. Are you open to it? How do you treat the true man or woman of God? You might need to adjust your thinking as Naaman did. Get God's heartbeat on this, and refuse to treat as common the ministries He has sent. The enemy of your soul seeks to disguise what is precious and present you with counterfeits that will leave you wanting. His hope is that you will reject the true servants of God in your midst and settle for fortune cookie substitutes and 40 years in the wilderness.

Hunger for the proceeding word of God. Believe the word of the authentic prophet and obey it, knowing that you will prosper. *Remember* that the widow of Zarephath and her son would have perished if she had rejected God's word through Elisha. *Remember* that if Naaman had washed in the filthy Jordan just once, his healing would have been lost. And *remember* that the destitute woman's sons would have been hauled off into slavery had she not gathered enough vessels to contain the riches of oil that made her solvent.

Allow God to bring you to the activation of your prophetic promise. Align yourself with His words and His ways, and He will take you to a new level of fulfillment, a place you have not yet seen, a place of prophetic prosperity in which life fires on all cylinders and your kingdom assignment is completed to His glory and the rejoicing of your heart.

Think on This

Are you familiar with the anointing, experientially speaking? How comfortable or uncomfortable are you with the subject of the anointing or with seeing yourself as an anointed person? Have you seen the integrity of the anointing protected? Left unguarded? Explain what your prophetic response looks like? Do you see yourself in the Bible characters mentioned? Where is prophetic prosperity evident in your life?

Notes

1. Biblesoft's *New Exhaustive Strong's Numbers and Concordance with Expanded Greek-Hebrew Dictionary.* CD-ROM. Biblesoft, Inc. and International Bible Translators, Inc. (© 1994, 2003, 2006) s.v. "dunamis," (NT 1411).
2. See Chapter 4.
3. Ibid., s.v. "epaggelia," (NT 1860).
4. See Genesis 12:7; 13:15; 15:7,18; 17:8; 26:4; 28:13; 50:24; Exodus 3:8; 6:8; Leviticus 20:24.

Chapter 7

Prophetic Words: Seasonal and Step-Ordering

Your ears shall hear a word behind you, saying, "This is the way, walk in it," whenever you turn to the right hand or whenever you turn to the left (Isaiah 30:21).

God is an always-speaking God who guides us every step of the way. In times of transition, tearing down, and building up, He speaks words that move the needle and support His timing. With the slightest nudge and in a myriad of ways, He illuminates who we are and who we are becoming. Yet, for all the creative ways in which He is able to reach us, His speaking falls into two broad categories: the *seasonal word* and the *step-ordering word.*

The seasonal word speaks to a point in our journey. It often comes at pivotal moments in which choices are most critical and confusing. A seasonal word helps us to clear the brush from the path and navigate these tricky intersections. When the "how to" or the "where next" seem unclear, the seasonal word serves as a bridge, straddling the gaps and carrying us forward during times of trial and transition.

The step-ordering word speaks throughout life's changing seasons. It acts as a divine North Star guiding us through the long arc of life and destiny fulfillment. Step-ordering words transcend seasonal shifts and help us to see them in the context of the bigger picture. They make sense of our life sequences and always keep us pointed to our destination.

Knowing the difference between seasonal and step-ordering words is extremely important. This understanding helps us to hone our prophetic response and improve our forward motion, in the short term and the long.

Different Seasons, Different Reasons

Remember that God's ways of speaking are unlimited. We know He speaks through His Word and through His prophets. In Chapter 1, we saw that He also speaks through dreams, visions, angels, and His still small voice. Every *God said* is stunning, although some are delivered more dramatically than others. When a prophet who does not know you walks up the aisle and calls you out, it will stop your clock. Yet regardless of how dramatic or subtle the form of prophetic utterance might be, it ought to get our attention.

Joel prophesied some of the means God would use to speak to us. Remember two things as we revisit the following passage: firsts are significant, and Joel's words as quoted by Peter were the first ones uttered in the opening salvo of the first sermon preached on the first day of the Church age:

> *And it shall come to pass in the last days, says God, that I will pour out of My Spirit on all flesh; your sons and your daughters shall prophesy, your young men shall see visions, your old men shall dream dreams. And on My menservants and on My maidservants I will pour out My Spirit in those days; and they shall prophesy* (Acts 2:17-18).

Apart from the varied prophetic vehicles named, this passage has seasonal implications—not in terms of season words as such, but in terms of the age groups mentioned. Before we search them out, let's first reiterate the context of Joel's broader points: First, the prophecy speaks to diversity and inclusion, and dismisses age, gender, and class biases. And secondly, the prophecy makes clear that all in the family of God shall prophesy.

Now let's consider the two clauses (in reverse order) in which Joel, under the inspiration of the Holy Spirit, addressed the seasons of life within the context of the prophetic.

1. *"your old men shall dream dreams"* (Acts 2:17).

2. *"your young men shall see visions"* (Acts 2:17).

Because God's Spirit was poured out on all flesh, the mention of men in these two statements is not meant to exclude or discriminate. Also, please note that the term *old men* is not age-related as much as it is a reference to maturity. The Greek word translated "old men" is *presbuteros,*[1] which also suggests church leadership. (It is the root from which Paul's mention of the presbytery in First Timothy 4:4 is taken.)[2]

Joel's point is that mature people tend to see the world in the broad context that comes from years of experience and learning. Their dreams are linked to a global perspective rather than a self-involved one. In other words, church elders have big-picture prophetic dreams that directly influence their leadership style and goals.

The term *young men* is a reference to youthfulness[3] that is intended to speak as much spiritually as physically. Think back for a moment to the three great revelations that begin to unfold when we come to Christ: first, His divinity; second, the sense of personal identity; and third, the understanding of personal destiny.

God speaks to the youthful as often and as loudly as He speaks to the mature, but He does it in an "age"-sensitive manner. When I was a young man, God helped me to understand who I was. He confirmed my giftings, office, and calling. The visions He gave me guided my maturation so that I could get beyond my insecurities and into the deeper waters of His plan for my life.

Today, my viewpoint is more global and less self-involved. The goal is no longer to figure out who I am, but to walk in the fullness of true apostolic and prophetic leadership. If finding myself were still the issue, I could not be effective in my current role. My ministry is firing on many cylinders at once; I do not have time to focus on the man in the mirror. That does not mean that God is done maturing me; it means that I am in a different season with different needs than in times past.

My conversations with Oral Roberts were so instructive in this area. As an elder in the Body of Christ, Oral dreamed the mature dreams Joel mentioned. He was not interested in talking about himself, but was preoccupied with what God was doing in the Church. The same is true of people like Reinhard Bonnke. Because their identities and kingdom positions are settled, they are not concerned with being recognized. Instead, with fire in their eyes, they grab us by the collar and say, "Here is what the Lord is telling me about the Church."

RESIST PROPHETIC LEGALISM

Seasonal aspects of the prophetic as revealed in Joel's prophecy are important but not restrictive. Trying to rigidly categorize them will cause spiritual paralysis and confusion. God speaks however He chooses to speak, in whatever manner and at any given time. For example, young Joseph—an unseasoned teen—received two weighty dreams that had enormous personal *and* global implications (see Gen. 37:5-9). Joseph was not yet a mature man able to implement the vision. He was a young man whose dreams would carry him through long years of tribulation, and then unfold exactly as God promised.

SEASONAL WORDS

Can you recall a crisis time when God dispelled your darkness with a single word, vision, or dream? Do you remember how it changed your outlook and gave you the strength to fight another day? He may have said something as simple as, "I am here. I have not forgotten you," yet it bridged the chasm you thought would swallow you whole.

That is what a seasonal prophetic word does: it carries you from Point A (a job loss, death of a loved one, betrayal, foreclosure, or an addiction) to Point B (your next opportunity, the healing of your grief, the willingness to trust again, the realization that your house is not your identity, the belief in God's ability to deliver you). The seasonal word builds a bridge across your transition.

In Chapter 5, I shared the testimony of my "speedily" miracles. While preaching from the Book of Psalms, a single verse lit up my heart: *"Answer me speedily, O Lord; my spirit fails! Do not hide Your face from me, lest I be like those who go down into the pit"* (Ps. 143:7).

At the time, I was dealing with two major issues—and I mean *major*. My wife and I battled one issue for five years; the other was almost a year old. The issues had taxed me beyond what I saw as my ability to cope. The level of distraction was overwhelming. I remember saying, "God, I can't take this anymore."

It was as simple as that. I needed a quick answer, but saw no natural way for it to manifest. Yet, as I ministered to others, God dropped Psalm 143:7 in my heart. It hit like a spiritual atom bomb—a missile from heaven that destroyed the strongholds and released divine resolution in a single strike.

The method of delivery was not the issue. God did not send one of His generals to announce, "Thus saith the Lord." It wasn't a dream, a vision, or an angel with a message from heaven. No. God rocked my world with a single, familiar verse of Scripture, and it was as powerful as any prophetic event I could imagine. That verse was rhema in the form of a seasonal word. In less than a week, the phone rang and the season had changed. Gayla and I were stunned by the transformation, but God wasn't. All He said was, "Didn't I tell you I was going to answer you speedily?"

God's seasonal word contradicted everything I knew about the situation and utterly defied the circumstances. That is the way it is with God—when He said, *"Let there be light"* (Gen. 1:3), there was no light present. His speaking refuted the status quo and altered reality, thus causing light to be.

If you want to be alert to seasonal and other prophetic words, you have to prepare yourself for the dichotomy between *what is* and what He says *will be.* If He speaks of blessing in the midst of your drought, do not expect the dry, cracked soil to validate His promise. If that is your measuring stick, you will discount the promise and discard your only ticket *out* of the drought. God's speaking does not mirror the situation—it revolutionizes it!

Step-Ordering Words

A step-ordering word (also known as a *life word*) is another sworn enemy of the status quo. Unlike the seasonal word, which guides you through a single transition, the step-ordering word overarches the span of your life.

Like steel girders upholding your identity and destiny, step-ordering words remain in position through all seasons. They never shift or yield under pressure, they stand firm regardless of the weather, and they refuse to conform to the ebb and flow of circumstances. A step-ordering word could address a calling to missions or marine biology or the pastorate. Or it could speak to your calling to comfort the hurting. Whatever the message of your step-ordering word, it will inform your choices and goals.

Life words are powerful and lasting, but do not only speak to vocation. When Jesus called Peter "the rock" (see Matt. 16:18), it was a life word. It cemented not only Peter's destiny, but also his identity. Peter needed to know who he was. Otherwise, he would spend the rest of his life swimming against the current of his destiny. Jesus's step-ordering word revealed the road from fisherman to fisher of men and freed the budding apostle to flow with the anointing that was on his life.

When Jesus called Peter "the rock" it was a life word. It cemented not only Peter's destiny, but also his identity.

FIGHT FOR YOUR WORD

Even with your life word tucked into your heart, you will face days of doubt and tribulation, as Peter did on the night Jesus was arrested (see Matt. 26:69-75). Dejected and ashamed, Peter returned to his fishing business. But his life word from Jesus kept working. In time, the lover of his soul brought Peter back into His fold (see Mark 16:7; John 21:15-19) and onto the road of ministry.

Every life is attached to a destiny. I guess that is why biographies fascinate me. Not long ago, I read about Hollywood stars John Wayne and Fred Astaire. The two men were as different as night and day, yet both were hugely successful entertainers—Wayne played the two-fisted man's man and Fred Astaire played the elegant and comedic gentleman. Each knew who he was and what worked for him.

I have no idea what these men's spiritual beliefs were. But Christian or not, each of them were unique. John Wayne was not created to be Fred Astaire, and Fred Astaire was no John Wayne. If they had traded identities, both would likely have failed miserably.

Like Wayne and Astaire, we have to get to the place where we are satisfied to be the people God created us to be. After some early hand wringing, I have accepted the fact that I was not called to deliver highly polished, tux-and-tails motivational sermons. I am more of a two-fisted prophet. I have compassion for people's situations, but I was not built to butter up the folks in the pews. My approach is more like, "Buck up, Pilgrim. I'm going to hit you with a word from heaven."

The step-ordering words that pointed me to the office of prophet have helped me to firm up rather than dress up my identity. I am settled in my assignment and my gifting. Even if I tried, I could not pull off the Fred Astaire thing. My *God said*—and yours—is unyielding and inescapable.

Whether you are a Wayne, an Astaire, or anybody else, the power of a single life word can carry you to your destiny. Yet God often gives us more than one. In my case, a second life word promising regional revival has created an unquenchable thirst in me. I believe the revival He showed me will usher in the Second Coming of the Lord. The vision has withstood the decades and has kept me standing against strong opposing currents for 25 years. It is part of my identity; I cannot relinquish it. Therefore, I continue to stand in position, no matter what the devil or anyone else says.

What step-ordering words has God spoken into your life? Do they govern your direction, or have they faded from view? It does not matter how far off course you think you have strayed, I guarantee that the road is still there. All you need is to remember who you are and what He has planned for you. Trust Him, and He will take you there.

STEP-ORDERING OR SEASONAL?

David was created by God to be Israel's king. The prophet Samuel *"took the horn of oil and anointed him in the midst of his brothers; and the Spirit of the Lord came upon David from that day forward"* (1 Sam. 16:13). This was David's step-ordering word. The big picture of his life was settled. His identity was clear. His destiny steps had been ordered by God, and David knew it.

Yet his predecessor's reign dragged on and David faced an uphill climb for years. When the Amalekites raided Ziklag and carried the people to captivity, David was devastated. Uncertain what to do, he looked up:

> *David inquired of the Lord, saying, "Shall I pursue this troop? Shall I overtake them?"*
>
> *And He answered him,* ***"Pursue, for you shall surely overtake them and without fail recover all"*** (1 Samuel 30:8).

This seasonal word was David's lifeline during a terrible crisis. It cleared his head, leveled out his emotions, and bridged the treacherous transition. His seasonal word was situation-specific, but it supported the life word that sealed his position as Israel's king. The rhema received at Ziklag assured David's success in the short term so that he could fulfill his long-term mission.

Prophetic Anchors

As we have already seen, our prophetic weapons were not designed to dazzle; they are for waging war. The prophetic is more than a heavenly pick-me-up. It provides spiritual anchors that keep us from drifting off course and out of God's will.

Never forget that the enemy is out to kill, steal, and destroy (see John 10:10). Creating misery is not his main line of work, but it facilitates his real goals, which are to undermine God's purposes and destroy destinies.

A chief demonic tactic is to create upheaval and doubt by sending counterfeit, confusing voices that speak just enough truth to keep us hooked while leading us astray. Often, these voices are in our own heads! When David first discovered the catastrophe at Ziklag, he and his men wept till their tear ducts ran dry. Imagine the thoughts racing through their minds, and the "what ifs" that weighed down their hearts.

As leader, David faced an additional threat *within his own camp.* Scripture reveals that *"the people spoke of stoning him"* (1 Sam. 30:6). It must surely have looked like the end of the line for David. And that is exactly what the enemy wanted him to think. He wanted to wear down God's chosen king to the point that he would voluntarily discard his life word.

David was in desperate need. So he sought God and received the seasonal word to "Pursue, overtake, and recover all" (see 1 Sam. 30:8). This succinct word anchored David and pressed him forward. Instead of succumbing to fear and discouragement, he tasted victory and moved closer to the throne.

Sometimes, a seasonal word is the difference between giving up and living to fight another day. Whether it carries you through a legal matter, a business negotiation, a rough patch in your marriage, or an illness, a seasonal word will carry you far enough to remind you of the bigger picture—your life word. When the two are fused together in your heart, you cannot be moved.

Bear in mind this truth: life's setbacks do not nullify your destiny. Ishmael's conception did not cancel the promise of Isaac. Slavery did not annul Joseph's prophetic destiny. Ziklag did not close the book on David's future as king. Your setbacks cannot seal an unwanted fate unless you allow them to.

Jesus's blood was not spilled just to save you from hell and ship you off to heaven. God has a distinct purpose for your being here. He has empowered you to impact the world. He has given you prophetic anchors to help you to steady your "ship" so that you will pursue, overtake, and recover all.

Encouraged and Strengthened

Psalm 22:3 says that God is *"enthroned in the praises of Israel."* David, the quintessential worshiper, understood this. When everything seemed lost and David had cried his last tear, Scripture says he *"encouraged himself in the Lord his God"* (1 Sam. 30:6 KJV).

Knowing David's reputation, we have to assume that he praised God at Ziklag. And, knowing that God inhabits His people's praises, we can also assume that His presence fell. What we sometimes forget is that God's voice accompanies His presence. So, by magnifying God, David opened a dialogue with Him, and God helped David to reconnect with his identity.

Imagine the conversation:

"David, I have appointed you king, and you *will* be king."

"I'm not feeling it, Lord. It would be tough to take the throne if these guys kill me first," David responds.

"David, *I AM,* and I say that you *will* be king."

David responds, "Either You will have to resurrect me or all my enemies will have to fail miserably. I'm not seeing either one happening."

"You ***will*** be king," God replies.

"An awful lot has to change, Lord...nevertheless, I trust You. Yes! I will be king. You have promised!"

By looking to the Author of the promise, David regained his strength and brought his *God said* front and center again. Ziklag would not be the last trial in his life; but always, David worshiped God, and always, he stayed on the prophetic road that was paved by the life word Samuel delivered when David was a boy.

This is a key to your becoming unmovable. If you will worship the Author of your promise, He will pull you through every form of adversity. He will repeat the promise over and over and over again until it is engrafted into your very being. When that happens, it will steel you against every opposing force hell and the world can muster.

STRENGTH AND WEAKNESS

To be discouraged is to be spiritually weakened and more vulnerable to attack. You can stay encouraged and spiritually strong by worshiping God and cleaving to His prophetic promises. They will remind you that *you are who God says you are*. Let His seasonal and step-ordering words anchor you, in good times as well as bad.

Real-Time, Real-Life Word

God's proceeding word will sustain you in every season. My father and millions of others experienced overwhelming adversity during the Great Depression. Yet even in the midst of that long season of scarcity, my father received a word from God!

One day, as he stood on a soup line hoping for a meal, the Lord said, "If you'll get out of this soup line and go out to your place of prayer (a certain place in the woods where my dad liked to pray), spread out your blanket, study My Word, and pray, I will show you how to prosper."

Empty stomach and all, my father left the soup line and did what the Lord instructed. That day, he learned from God what Oral Roberts would call the seed-faith principle. God revealed to my dad the workings of the tithe and showed him how to live a prosperous life.

Before your eyes glaze over because you know all about tithing, let me remind you that God was speaking about prosperity to a man standing in a soup line. Talk about an out-of-season word!

My dad caught the revelation and began operating in it. The Lord blessed him more and more. Dad prospered and shared the revelation at every church he pastored. Thousands were affected by the yoke-breaking, poverty-ending power of it. They learned that God makes a way for tithers even when all hell seems positioned against them.

Dad had hellish seasons still to come. Because of corporate dishonesty, my parents' investments, including their life savings for retirement, were completely wiped out, leaving them broke.

I was still living at home at the time, and I remember how we lived day to day and nickel to nickel.

But here's the remarkable thing: when Dad learned that his retirement account was lost, the first thing he did was write out his tithe check. Some people would say that is *crazy.* But my dad had received a step-ordering word from God regarding the tithe. He knew it was pivotal to his destiny.

The devil, of course, will test a word like that! He always challenges the believer's commitment by asking, "Did God *really* say that to you?" (see Gen. 3:1).

Not only did my dad believe God had said it, but he preached it himself. Don't you know that Satan wanted to discredit God's Word and the vessel He used to preach it? Thank God Dad saw through the enemy's strategy. He knew that God had raised him up to deliver people from poverty, so he refused to back down.

People thought Dad had lost his mind. I thought so too. I asked him, "Dad, what are we going to do now that everything is lost?"

He said, "The first thing I'm going to do is pay the tithe. All I've got is what came in this week but, bless God, I'm tithing on it." Dad trusted the Lord to protect and preserve him. He knew God and he knew who he was in Him. Dad would not relinquish his identity or let go of the promise over his life. As serious as the crisis was, Dad knew he was not defenseless, nor was he a victim—he stood his ground and saw his life restored!

God's prophetic promises—His seasonal and step-ordering words—are powerful. Through every trial, God speaks. He is speaking to you even now. Listen intently for the sound of His voice. Ask Him for answers, just as David did. Set aside whatever you must in order to hear Him speak. And always remember that you live by every unfailing word that proceeds from God's mouth.

Think on This

Do you identify more with the "old men" or the "young men" in Joel's prophecy? Explain. In what ways does this season of your life seem to fit or not fit the life word(s) God has spoken to you? Describe the most recent seasonal word God has given you. How has that word helped you? Describe what you consider to be the most defining step-ordering (life) word God has spoken to you.

Notes

1. Biblesoft's *New Exhaustive Strong's Numbers and Concordance with Expanded Greek-Hebrew Dictionary*. CD-ROM. Biblesoft, Inc. and International Bible Translators, Inc. (© 1994, 2003, 2006) s.v. "presbuteros," (NT 4245).
2. Ibid., s.v. "presbuterion," (NT 4244).
3. Ibid., s.v. "neaniskos," (NT 3495).

Chapter 8

Prophesying in Proportion to Your Faith

For I say, through the grace given unto me, to every man that is among you, not to think of himself more highly than he ought to think; but to think soberly, according as God hath dealt to every man the measure of faith. For as we have many members in one body, and all members have not the same office: so we, being many, are one body in Christ, and every one members one of another. Having then gifts differing according to the grace that is given to us, whether prophecy, let us ***prophesy according to the proportion of faith*** (Romans 12:3-6 KJV).

Many members...one body...multiple gifts. God's Spirit is poured out on *all* flesh. Yet, unity does not imply uniformity. The gifts function according to the grace and the proportion of faith we possess as individuals. This diversity strengthens us. By it the house of God is edified, meaning it is built up, established, and emboldened.[1]

Keep in mind the distinct and separate meanings of *"your sons and daughters shall prophesy"* (Joel 2:28) and *"He Himself gave some to be...prophets"* (Eph. 4:11). The first statement refers to the outpouring of the Holy Spirit upon God's prophetic army, while the second refers to the giving of specific leadership gifts. Men and women called to the office of prophet not only prophesy but *are* prophets—fivefold ministers who bear a heavy burden of responsibility and are subject to a high level of scrutiny. They are called to speak, often into weighty matters; therefore, their prophetic track records must be scrupulously assessed.

This chapter is about the distinctions in gifting. My intent is to eliminate confusion and empower believers to move in the gifts without hindrance and in direct proportion to their individual faith. This clarification will help us distinguish spiritually silly, lawless, false "prophets" from those who are called of God to love and nourish His Church.

The Proportion of Faith

An analogy will help us to see the various levels at which spiritual gifts operate. Think about an occasion when you or someone in your family was sick. How did you handle the need? Did you take your position of spiritual authority and pray for the sick person? Or did you ask your favorite healing evangelist to fly in and do it for you?

Having a sick person prayed over by someone with a gift like Kathryn Kuhlman or Smith Wigglesworth would be wonderful. Certain people are powerfully anointed in the area of healing. But they don't necessarily live at your house. *But you do.* Therefore, my guess is that you relied on your measure of faith and you prayed.

Now let's assume that your prayers were marvelously answered. Did your success prompt you to rent out an arena and hold a massive healing service? The answer is probably not, unless the healing ministry is your God-ordained calling and you have been maturing in it for some time.

Every believer is called to pray for the sick. What distinguishes most Christians from Benny Hinn is a matter of proportion: Benny Hinn has been set apart by God for the healing ministry. He is one of God's "generals" in that realm, and the faith in which he operates is proportional to his assignment.

Now apply the analogy to the prophetic. Joel prophesied that *all* would prophesy. That means *all.* Yet, not all are called in the same way. Some are set apart by God to prophesy at a high level of magnitude and accountability. They don't just prophesy; they are prophets—to nations, destinies, cities, churches, and leaders. They are sent by God to plow specific prophetic roadways and release specific prophetic direction.

A high level of faith is required for the office of prophet. Moral excellence, prophetic accuracy, precise articulation, and boldness are critical to the mission. Not everyone is called to operate at that level in the prophetic realm. That does not mean that others whose central callings are focused elsewhere cannot be used as God's mouthpieces in the course of their everyday lives. God raised all of us to be oracles in our spheres of influence. We are His mouthpieces in our homes, businesses, schools, and communities. And we are called to speak in proportion to our faith.

Mind the Measure

If you have ever spent time with a friend who is experiencing adversity, you have probably sensed the prompting of the Holy Spirit to utter a word of encouragement. I am not talking about saying something nice to help your friend feel better. I am talking about being God's mouthpiece. He might tell you to say, "This situation will not end the way it began," or "God has heard your prayer." Whatever He leads you to say, it will bring light to the situation.

During a service at our church not too long ago, God pointed out a certain woman and prompted me to speak to her. What I started out saying sounded similar to what you might tell a struggling friend; but when I called her out, I did not yet have the whole picture. That would probably make most people nervous, but when I am moving in my calling as a prophet, there is no fear or doubt. Instead, there is certainty and boldness in obeying Him.

I told the woman what He told me to say: "God has heard and is answering your prayers." The statement does not sound particularly profound. Yet when I said it, the woman exploded into tears. God then began to speak pointedly through the word of knowledge. I mentioned a certain list she had written out—a literal list with a specific number of items. No one but she and God knew the list existed.

God had her attention, and continued by saying that He was going to move in a miraculous way in her life. Unlike the list He mentioned, this statement sounds fairly general to us, but in the context of all He said, it was hugely impactful to the woman. The prophecy served both as a seasonal word that bridged whatever crisis she was in, and as a step-ordering word with lifelong implications.

There is a proportion of faith required to deliver a word like this. If the messenger operates outside the measure and the calling, there is no telling "who" is speaking. Not only that, but a precious child of God, who is searching for answers and may already be hurting, is put at great risk.

That is an example of the prophetic going off the rails. Remember that there is a price paid by genuine prophets who hear His voice at the level of the fivefold office. These men and women continue to pay the price after the prophecies are released. It is not a realm for the cavalier or seekers of the limelight. Prophesying is not about the one prophesying; it is about the proceeding word of God.

For the false or misguided "prophet," it is about self. They are often insecure people who want to impress others or make a name for themselves. They sometimes rely on educated guesses about the people to whom they prophesy. They may feel safe in judging situations by people's countenance or dress. What an abomination this is! Opinions and observations have nothing to do with what God is saying. God does not call His prophets to react to appearances, but to the unseen realm that He chooses to reveal. That is where real prophetic ministry begins.

To prophesy in proportion to your faith means to go no further than your mandate. Unless God has called you to the office of prophet, you must realize that the friend or stranger before you is not under your spiritual authority. Although you are authorized to issue words that edify, exhort, or comfort, you are not called to speak to the person's future choices, for example. To exceed the bounds of your mandate will produce nothing more than confusion and quite possibly destruction.

I have no desire to quench any believer's rightful ministry. It is my hope that everyone in the Body of Christ would be used to their fullest capacity in God. It is critical, however, that we function at the level of our callings. God does not look away when His gifts are misused or when His people are drawn into deception by imposters. These are serious matters and He will deal with them.

Watch Your Step-Ordering

Unless you are called to the office of a prophet, I strongly advise against issuing step-ordering words to anyone. Absent the call to the prophetic office, you do not have the authority to offer such direction. It is not up to you to tell the woman in the pew behind you that she should begin packing for the mission field or buying her future wedding dress. As spiritual as such proclamations might sound, they become a source of confusion and they dishonor God.

Step-ordering words are the domain of the prophetic office. When God releases a prophet to serve, He releases someone mature, seasoned, tried, tested, and found to be honorable in the things of the Spirit. Through these servants, He then releases step-ordering words that directly impact lives and cause people or groups of people to act on what was spoken.

This is why it is so important to judge prophecy. Leaders must strike a delicate balance in wisely stewarding the flow of the gifts. Ideally, in any church or meeting, leaders will judge prophecy before it is released, as it is their responsibility to prevent deceptive words from becoming guiding principles to unsuspecting victims. No one should be permitted to prophesy beyond their level of authority. Those in authority must be willing to prevent such attempts, whether from false prophets and/or misguided ones.

The Prophet's Proportion

The fivefold-ministry prophet is authorized and equipped to set life words in motion. A few years ago, after ministering at a large church in San Jose, California, I was unexpectedly invited to preach at another church's midweek service. It was in the summertime, as I recall, and a typical summertime crowd showed up: me, the pastor, and a handful of the faithful.

Nothing particularly earth shattering occurred until the Holy Spirit gave me an incisive word for the pastor. I told him that God was getting ready to open up a new facility for the church and that he (the pastor) would negotiate the deal. Then I said something I could not have known: "Your natural tendency is to hire an attorney and get a realtor or someone else to help you with this deal. That would make common sense. It would be the way I would look at it too. But the Lord said that you are the negotiator and the spirit of negotiation is upon you." The prophecy ended with a specific detail: "Act quickly and move fast when the door opens." This was a loaded step-ordering word. I prayed for the pastor, the service closed, and I went on my way.

A few days later, he found a property. With the prophecy in mind, he called the owner, who happened to be a Jewish man.

"I'd like to lease your property with an option to buy," said the pastor.

The owner replied with a question: "How much do you want to give me for the lease?"

The pastor offered a figure and listened as the man worked up some numbers on his calculator. After checking the math, the owner said, "OK. Now, what will you offer for the property if we proceed with the option to buy?"

Convinced by the prophecy that he was anointed to negotiate and act quickly, the pastor threw back a number, to which the gentleman responded, "That sounds like a doable deal."

The pastor quickly went to his board and updated them on the deal he had negotiated. The board members responded predictably: "Let's get the attorneys and a real estate agent involved. We need to handle this situation with caution."

They probably did not expect the pastor's rapid-fire response: "What did the man of God say? He said the spirit of negotiation is on me and I need to move quickly. We're going to obey our 'thus saith the Lord'!"

The board caught the vision and released the pastor to move forward with the deal. Meanwhile, the Jewish man who owned the property called and asked him, "Are you serious about this?"

The pastor assured him that he was. The man tested his commitment with a new hypothetical. "Let's say the price was a million dollars.[2] Would you still be interested?"

The pastor stood firm. "Yes, sir, I would."

The man said, "I've just been offered double that amount."

"Oh," was all the pastor could say.

"But," the man went on, "I gave you my word."

The pastor began to see why negotiating the deal himself mattered. The owner was willing to settle for far less money because he had a verbal agreement with the man of God and would not violate it.

This step-ordering word played out exactly as God said. I recently visited the church and found it bursting at the seams. They have to run four weekend services to meet the need. An articulate and precise step-ordering word released God's plan. It was an effective word spoken through a tested prophet; and because it was acted upon, it prospered.

The "Prophetic Trinity" Test

The fundamental test for the gamut of prophetic utterances is found in First Corinthians 14:3: *"But he who prophesies speaks* ***edification*** *and* ***exhortation*** *and* ***comfort*** *to men."* This verse applies to those who stand in the office of prophet and those who do not. These requirements do not imply that every authentic prophetic word will be silky sweet. Prophecies do not always pat people on the back and sing their praises. There are times when God brings a stronger, more corrective tone. He might even rebuke! But the end result is always the same: edification, exhortation, and comfort.

Strong words are not meant to add to people's misery, but to encourage them toward virtue. For example, if you are in a damaging relationship with a man who is not your husband, a word of rebuke might not seem particularly comforting until it saves you from utter destruction.

The purpose of prophecy is revealed by Paul's chosen vocabulary. *Edification,* as mentioned earlier, involves building.

Because it builds people, it strengthens them against life's storms. It also advances God's agenda and produces spiritual increase. God's building process is always to our benefit and the furtherance of His kingdom.

The word *exhortation* covers a lot of territory and includes the following meanings:

> 1) a calling near, summons, (esp. for help)
>
> 2) impartation, supplication, entreaty
>
> 3) exhortation, admonition, encouragement
>
> 4) consolation, comfort, solace; that which affords comfort or refreshment.[3]

God's exhortation is His offer of help and an encouragement toward moral excellence. He entreats us to move in the direction of our identity in Him and admonishes us to live His way. Exhortation refreshes us with His guidance and urges us to be the men and women He created us to be.

The Greek word translated *comfort* (see 1 Cor. 14:3) is also lush with meaning. It denotes:

> 1. any address, whether made for the purpose of persuading, or of arousing and stimulating, or of calming and consoling
>
> a) consolation, comfort[4]

When God speaks, He comforts and refreshes us. His words bring consolation; they relieve our pressures and distress. He never adds insult to injury, but brings healing deep within. His speaking creates, not confusion, but calmness.

When you have truly heard from God, you are strengthened within. This is why David wrote: *"For by You I can run against a troop, by my God I can leap over a wall"* (Ps. 18:29). If a prophecy leaves you feeling beaten down, you have to ask yourself, "Was it really from God?"

Pinpointing Edification, Exhortation, and Comfort

A realistic hypothetical can help us to see the elements of the prophetic trinity. Imagine that a woman named Mary Lou has come to a special service at which a proven prophet is ministering. Mary Lou has just been through an emotional trauma. Her heart is broken and she is finding it hard to recover and move on.

Mary Lou is seated halfway to the rear of the sanctuary when the prophet calls her out and asks her name. Immediately, he begins to prophesy: "Mary Lou, there is a strengthening being poured out by God into your life right now. It will cause you to rise up and be the woman He has called you to be."

Right off the bat, the prophet exhorts Mary Lou. His words encourage her to draw near for God's help and to see herself as being all she was created to be. He continues to prophesy, saying, "There are some things that God has already dealt with through the dreams and visions He has given you. I am here to tell you by the Holy Spirit that He will make a way where there seems to be no way."

The prophet edifies Mary Lou by addressing her unspoken despair. His words serve to build her up, strengthening and establishing her. They remind her that God has not forsaken her.

The prophet ends by saying, "I sense that your heart is broken, but I want you to know that He heals the brokenhearted. The sadness and discouragement are going to lift. Your dark season is coming to a close."

The prophet closes by bringing comfort. Mary Lou knows that God sees her pain and is bringing the remedy for which she longs. Under the unction of the Holy Spirit, the prophet has announced a welcome end to her affliction. God has used him to refresh her soul, dispel confusion, and console her in her time of need.

If we are sensitive to the opportunities around us and will develop hearing ears, we can be used by God to meet people right where they are. Ministry will not always involve a five-pound leather-bound Bible and a recitation of the Roman Road. It *will*, however, always involve listening and responding in wisdom so that we can penetrate the darkness and make prophetic deposits of His love. The well-dressed woman ahead of you in the checkout line might look like she has it all together. Although she might not cry out for help, she may very well be at a breaking point in her life, and you may very well have been sent by God to meet her there.

God did not create and save you to leave you powerless. You were birthed to bring transformation to others.

Do you remember the woman at the well in the 4th chapter of the Gospel of John? She saw Jesus but did not address Him. She said nothing about her troubled life, but He discerned it. He saw her need and opened the conversation.

Then, with a word of knowledge about the many men in her life, He turned on the light in her heart. He did not reveal everything He knew about her, because drawing attention to her sin was not His ultimate purpose. Instead, He said just enough to trigger her restoration. In a few moments, He lifted her out of her shame and into freedom. His speaking penetrated her heart to the point that His love spread throughout her community.

DON'T MINIMIZE THE OPPORTUNITY

We are surrounded by opportunities to speak life to others. Often, we overlook them because:

- We forget that God has given us power and authority to break yokes.
- We overestimate the obstacles because we are self-reliant rather than God-reliant.
- We lose sight of the world outside our four walls.
- We assume that "dry bones" cannot live again.

If we will ask God to give us hearing ears and discerning spirits, He will cause us to meet people at their point of need. If we will remember that He has *already* empowered to bless others, He will use us in amazing ways.

DAD AND "JACK"

Some ministry opportunities are more informal than even Jesus's encounter at the well. When I was a kid, my dad befriended our neighbor. Whenever we couldn't find Dad, we knew he was at the man's house playing gin rummy. Some might ask, "But wasn't your dad a preacher? Did he really play cards with the neighbor? Shouldn't he have been preaching to the man?"

Here is more fodder for religious indignation: The man (we'll call him Jack) smoked like a chimney and drank hard liquor. Every other word out of his mouth was an expletive. That did not stop Dad from being a friend to him. Instead, Dad listened patiently to Jack's troubles and encouraged him whenever they were together.

When Jack suffered a severe heart attack, Dad went straight to the hospital and asked, "How are you doing, Jack?"

Jack wasted no time blurting out his request: "Pray for me!"

In the past Jack had made it clear that prayer was not his thing. When Dad heard his request, he wanted to be sure he'd heard it right, so he asked, "What was that, Jack?"

"Pray for me. I need God to help me. I've made fun of you and given you a hard time now and again, but it never bothered you. You just kept telling me about the good things God does and how He heals people. Please—please, pray for me."

Dad laid his hand on Jack's chest and the power of God hit the man, from the top of his head to the soles of his feet. Later, Jack's doctors were at a loss to explain what happened. They knew Jack had suffered a massive heart attack and should have suffered irreparable damage to the heart tissue. But he didn't. In fact, they found virtually no damage at all!

All that time, as Dad played cards with Jack, he edified, exhorted, and comforted him. It did not look like prophetic ministry, but it was. Dad ministered the love of Christ to Jack, and it opened the door of his heart.

Opportunities Everywhere

God is never at a loss to reach people. Once, shortly after boarding a plane, I noticed that the woman seated next to me was paying exceptionally close attention to the safety film that ran as we backed away from the gate. She seemed tense and laser-focused. She noted all the emergency procedures, located her life vest and the nearest emergency exit, and read every word on the safety card she found in the seatback in front of her.

I've heard the expression, "There are no atheists in foxholes." Well, there aren't any in planes either! Clearly, the woman was terrified. As we awaited takeoff, her eyes welled up with tears. When we hit turbulence, she freaked out altogether and began sobbing. I remember thinking, *There goes my crossword and a quiet afternoon off.*

I leaned over and said, "Ma'am, are you all right?"

"I'm terrified of flying!" she exclaimed.

I had figured out as much. As I began calmly speaking to her, God revealed some things. I said, "Ma'am, God has a purpose for your life and He is going to keep His hand upon you. You have a great heart for people—a great heart of compassion."

She said, "That's right! I'm on my way to see my daughter, even though I hate to fly."

I continued: "God is going to bring you through this thing. He is with you."

What was I doing? I was comforting, exhorting, and edifying her. Before I knew it, she'd told me all about her family, her Catholicism, and her uncertain eternal destination. By the time we landed, she was born again and filled with peace—all because I set aside my crossword puzzle and allowed God to reach her through me.

Opportunities like this are found everywhere we go. People are more willing to be reached than we realize. Often, they are open to any help they can find. Now, if you asked a stranger, "May I prophesy to you?" he or she might run in the opposite direction. But we can pray prophetically and allow God to edify, exhort, and comfort them.

We are equipped to move in the prophetic in any environment. Sometimes, our prophetic opportunities are for our protection. For example, if you own a business, He will give you the discerning of spirits so that you can counsel, hire, and fire with wisdom. He will give you words that speak life to your staff and operation. If you are unequally yoked with people whose presence constrains your company's potential, He will show you who needs to go. I often tell business owners, "You may be one firing away from the increase you have been praying to see."

A Seeing Anointing

Prophesying in proportion to our faith involves recognizing our gifts and operating within them. That is what the finest athletes do. They understand what it means to play within themselves. They know there is only one John Elway or one Michael Phelps. Likewise, there is only one me and one you. We do not get to choose our gifts, but if we use them wisely, our lives will be fruitful.

Prophetic gifts vary widely. When I talk about prophesying in proportion to one's faith, it is not strictly about words. My wife, Gayla, has what I call a *seeing anointing.* Whereas I operate primarily from the hearing-and-speaking realm, Gayla has brightly-colored, surround-sound dreams and visions through which God speaks very precisely to her.

Sometimes He uses visual images that provide direction as to specific tasks and assignments for Gayla's team. Often, her meeting topics are birthed in prophetic dreams or visions. Once, when we attended a Colorado Rockies' game, God spoke to Gayla as rain began falling. Instantly, He revealed the theme for her next women's meeting: "When It Rains, It Pours."

God's ways are limitless. His Spirit distributes all kinds of anointing. All we need to do is listen for His voice in whatever way He chooses to reveal it, and respond in whatever way He directs. No matter what He calls us to do—whether it looks spiritual or not—we need His anointing and His direction. If we minister, and especially if we prophesy, in proportion to our faith, there *will* be a glorious harvest.

Think on This

Describe the proportion of your faith in regard to the prophetic. What do you believe to be your role in God's prophetic army? Describe an experience and the impact of someone operating outside the proportion of their faith. What is your perspective about offering step-ordering words in the future? Have you ever received a prophecy that failed the edification, exhortation, and comfort test? What effect did it have?

Notes

1. Biblesoft's *New Exhaustive Strong's Numbers and Concordance with Expanded Greek-Hebrew Dictionary*,

CD-ROM, Biblesoft, Inc. and International Bible Translators, Inc. (1994, 2003, 2006) "oikodomeo," (NT 3618) and s.v. "oikodome," (NT 3619). See also Merriam-Webster Online, *Merriam-Webster Online Dictionary 2012,* s.v. "edify," http://www.merriam-webster.com/dictionary/edify (accessed January 30, 2012).

2. I no longer recall the exact figure. One million dollars may or may not be accurate, but you get the idea.
3. *Blue Letter Bible,* Dictionary and Word Search for *"paraklēsis"* (Strong's 3874), 1996-2012, http://www.blueletterbible.org/lang/lexicon/lexicon.cfm?Strongs=G3874&t=KJV (accessed January 30, 2012).
4. Ibid., s.v. *"paramythia"* (Strong's 3889), Blue Letter Bible, 1996-2012, http://www.blueletterbible.org/lang/lexicon/lexicon.cfm?Strongs=G3889&t=KJV (accessed January 30, 2012).

Chapter 9

Multigenerational Blessing

Then Israel saw Joseph's sons, and said, "Who are these?" And Joseph said to his father, "They are my sons, whom God has given me in this place." And he said, "Please bring them to me, and I will bless them" (Genesis 48:8-9).

When Jacob and his son, Joseph, were reunited in Egypt, the nation of Israel consisted of one extended family—fewer than 80 people! God's promise to Abraham's generations had barely begun to unfold; the enormous population He foretold was still in the future. Yet Jacob clung to the fulfillment of the promise, knowing it would not come to pass in his lifetime.

Jacob guarded the family's spiritual legacy and made sure his progeny did the same. On his deathbed, he reiterated the promise and spoke the blessing over Joseph's sons, who had been born in Egypt. He said:

> *God, before whom my fathers Abraham and Isaac walked, the God who has fed me all my life long to this day, the Angel who has redeemed me from all evil, bless the lads; let my name be named upon them, and the name of my fathers Abraham and Isaac; and let them grow into a multitude in the midst of the earth* (Genesis 48:15-16).

In the boys' hearing, Jacob summarized the history of the promise and his own experience with God, and spoke to its future implications. Abraham's generation had a stunning history. Descended from idolaters, they now worshiped the Most High God and were destined by Him to bless the whole earth. They were not born-again people, but they were not under the law either. Hundreds of years before the law was given, Abraham *"believed in the Lord, and He accounted it to him for righteousness"* (Gen. 15:6). Abraham's believing set generations of blessing in motion.

Jacob and Israel, Natural Man and Spiritual

Years before his trek to Egypt, Jacob had an unexpected wrestling match with God (see Gen. 32:24-31). It was a pivotal event after which God transformed Jacob's identity, saying, ***"Your name shall no longer be called Jacob, but Israel;*** *for you have struggled with God and with men, and have prevailed"* (Gen. 32:28).

The natural man, Jacob, was a schemer who worked hard to force his way on others (see Gen. 25:26,30; 27:5-29). The name *Jacob* literally means "supplanter."[1] It aptly described the natural man and his tendencies. But his new name represented the spiritual man he had become: *Israel,* which means "God prevails."[2] This was the real man, the spirit within that was designed to rise above Jacob's humanity.

Recognizing the ascendancy of spirit over flesh is an important key to transferring the blessing from one generation to the next. The Bible illustrates this point in a tender and consequential moment that occurred just before Jacob blessed his progeny and departed the earth:

> *Now it came to pass after these things that Joseph was told, "Indeed your father is sick"; and he took with him his two sons, Manasseh and Ephraim.* ***And Jacob was told,*** *"Look, your son Joseph is coming to you";* ***and Israel strengthened himself and sat up on the bed*** (Genesis 48:1-2).

Jacob, the natural man, was dying. Yet, Israel, the spiritual man, gathered his strength, sat up, and took care of business. His final opportunity to transfer the blessing had arrived and he would not miss it. Through his prophetic words and actions, Israel passed the torch and ensured the continuation of his family's multigenerational blessing.

Israel understood his role: he was not a container for the blessing, but a conduit. A container could have taken the blessing to the grave and let his generations fend for themselves. Israel would not; he would not die with God's heavenly deposit locked inside his remains. Instead, he would impart his dreams, visions, revelation, anointing, and giftings to his descendants, ensuring that his natural bloodline would not only inherit his wealth, but also the blessing underlying it.

The spiritual man, Israel, invigorated Jacob, whose earthly moments were numbered. Before addressing the future of his children and their progeny, Israel brought the covenant with God front and center:

> *Then Jacob said to Joseph: "God Almighty appeared to me at Luz in the land of Canaan and blessed me, and said to me, 'Behold, I will make you fruitful and multiply you, and I will make of you a multitude of people, and give this land to your descendants after you as an everlasting possession'"* (Genesis 48:3-4).

You cannot pass on what you do not own. Jacob lived in possession of the blessing and was ready to hand it off. Although he had prospered, his material wealth was nothing compared with what Joseph had amassed through his service to Pharaoh. The blessing of the natural man was not what Jacob's generations needed. What they needed was the blessing that had been passed down from Abraham. Therefore, *"Israel strengthened himself and sat up on the bed"* (Gen. 48:2), and imparted it.

> *Recognizing the ascendancy of spirit over flesh is an important key to transferring the blessing from one generation to the next.*

Beware of Tradition

For the blessing to be multigenerational, it takes intentionality and a willingness to embrace the ways of the Spirit over those of human tradition. When Joseph brought his sons to Jacob, the patriarch broke with custom: instead of placing his right hand on the eldest, he crossed his hands so the younger boy would receive the greater blessing. Jacob then proclaimed the blessing that we read earlier from Genesis 48:15-16.

Joseph reacted strongly to Israel's seeming mistake:

> *It displeased him; so he took hold of his father's hand to remove it from Ephraim's head to Manasseh's head. And Joseph said to his father, "Not so, my father, for this one is the firstborn; put your right hand on his head."*
>
> *But his father refused and said, "I know, my son, I know. He also shall become a people, and he also shall be great; but truly his younger brother shall be greater than he, and his descendants shall become a multitude of nations"* (Genesis 48:17-19).

Traditions will not work for God's prophetic generation. God will not be bound by them and neither should we. God will lay His hand upon whomever He chooses. Some of the "younger sons" will walk in the greater portion that most people see (from a religious perspective) as belonging to someone else.

We see this principle many times throughout Scripture. When God sent Samuel to anoint Israel's king, He did not release the prophet to anoint the most obvious candidate. The older, stronger, more forceful sons of Jesse (seven of them!)

failed to make God's cut. Instead, He chose the youngest, a ruddy shepherd boy forgotten in the fields (see 1 Sam. 16).

God's ways are truly not ours. When He sought someone to deliver Israel from Midianite oppression, he chose Gideon, a cowering man who said, *"O my Lord, how can I save Israel? Indeed my clan is the weakest in Manasseh, and I am the least in my father's house"* (Judg. 6:15). Yet God made Gideon to be a conqueror—his routing of the Midianites led to 40 years of peace!

The more we seek God's heart, the more we will think and act like Him. As a prophetic generation, we need to check our mindsets; we must be wary of traditions that resist the *now* move of His Spirit. Always, we must follow Him.

Multigenerational Perspective

Multigenerational blessing is always connected to covenant. Jacob understood that God's covenant with Abraham had not yet been fulfilled. Jacob knew the history of the promise and was as fully persuaded of it as Abraham had been. He knew God's prophetic proclamation had to have multigenerational implications.

Hindsight may be 20/20, but foresight is much more powerful. The patriarchs saw beyond the circumstances that so starkly contrasted the promises of God. The writer of Hebrews states, *"These all died in faith, not having received the promises, but having seen them afar off were assured of them, embraced them and confessed that they were strangers and pilgrims on the earth"* (Heb. 11:13). Consider the physical evidence they saw:

- Abraham: the first generation—the only proof he had of God's promise was a single son named Isaac.
- Isaac: the second generation—all he had to show were two sons, Esau and Jacob, who were both estranged.
- Jacob: the third generation—he had 12 sons and their offspring to show for the promise.
- The fourth generation—in Israel's days in Goshen, Joseph saw a seedling nation. But he lived to see three generations after him (see Gen. 50:23).

Strong physical evidence of God's promise would not be seen until 400 years later, when Israel numbered in the millions. At the time of the Exodus, the children of Israel were *"more and mightier than* [the Egyptians]" (Exod. 1:9). Yet even Moses saw only a partial manifestation of the promise that continues to unfold today.

If any of these men of God had viewed the promise in terms of their own lifetimes, the blessing would have ended with them. I cannot stress this enough: we must take the long view—the eternal view—of our *God said.* If we do, we will be mindful to preserve the blessing in our generation and share it with the next.

Age-Old Schemes

Even after they numbered in the millions, the Hebrews backed away from God's promise to Abraham. The ten spies saw living proof of the promise when they surveyed the Promised

Land. Yet, in fear and unbelief, they refused to take the land (see Num. 13–14).

It would not be the last time Israel backslid. After her exploits under Joshua, Israel fell into apostasy once again. With Joshua dead and buried, *"all that generation had been gathered to their fathers, **another generation arose after them who did not know the Lord nor the work which He had done for Israel**"* (Judg. 2:10).

The devil's time-tested strategy is to wage war against our children and grandchildren. He is successful against them when we (and, therefore, *they*) lose sight of the promise of God. We do this by becoming so self-absorbed as to forget that the promise can take longer than our lifetimes to fulfill. When it does not happen *now,* we tacitly accept Satan's suggestion that the promise is dead. So he attacks our progeny, in essence, trying to finish off the promise altogether.

Think back to King David's reign. God removed Saul and broke the curse that plagued Israel. Imperfect as David was, Israel enjoyed tremendous blessing under his rule—they prevailed in war and amassed great wealth. When David died, his son Solomon took the throne. He also began his reign well. He asked God for wisdom and He granted him every conceivable blessing (see 1 Kings 3:4-15). Solomon became even wealthier than his father, and Israel lived in peace under his rule.

Yet Solomon eventually lost the vision, led Israel into idolatry, and was warned by God of the judgment that would result after his death (see 1 Kings 11:1-13). When his son Rehoboam took the throne, Israel was divided in two. Because his father failed to guard the generational blessing, Rehoboam did not value it either. The great and powerful nation of Israel was fractured. Generations of decay followed and ended with both kingdoms being sacked.

The enemy took his opportunities where he found them. He could not stop David: lions and bears could not kill him, Saul could not kill him, and even Goliath was helpless against him. So the enemy went after David's children and grandchildren. There he found open doors and succeeded over time in taking God's people captive.

If we fail, as Solomon did, to protect and promote the blessing, we will truncate its multigenerational potential. Although we might not live to see the full impact, our descendants and our world will pay the price.

Break the Curse

The blessing is meant to be passed on, and God has equipped us to do it. Not only can we walk in the faith of the patriarchs, but we also have the benefit of a better covenant (see Heb. 7:22; 8:6). Because of the finished work of the cross, we who accept Christ as Savior and Lord have been granted the new birth. We are brand new creations whose spiritual DNA has been divinely re-engineered.

Bloodlines are important. Many books have been written on the subject of generational curses. It is a topic worthy of our attention. Yet, as born-again people, we should be far more focused on the blessing than we are on the curses. If the devil can inflict a curse on three or four generations in a family (see Exod. 34:7), think of what the work of the cross has accomplished! Even if 20 generations of alcoholics preceded you, a single drop of Jesus's shed blood is sufficient to deliver your bloodline and eradicate *any* curse.

It is up to us to answer the curse and appropriate the blessing. For multigenerational blessing to become reality in our families, someone (let it be us!) must be willing to rise up and break the curse. But how? By saying, "It doesn't matter how many fruits and nuts are in my family tree; the curse stops here, in *my* generation. I am not an addict; nor are my children, their children, or their children's children addicts. We are not bipolar or schizophrenic; we are not cheaters, liars, or sexual deviants. This family is blessed and all of our generations are blessed in Him, in Jesus's matchless name!"

CURSED OR CURSE-BREAKER?

As a born-again child of the King, you have two choices: You can submit to your family history and endure the curse that plagued your forbears, or you can be the curse-breaker who plows the prophetic path of blessing for generations to come. Remember, you are no longer a Jacob, but an Israel—a child of God ruled by the Spirit and not the flesh.

If you have children or plan to start a family, determine right now to be a natural *and* spiritual parent. Of course, your parenting should promote your children's physical, mental, and emotional well-being. But you are also to create a path in the spirit realm that generates blessing, vision, gifts, freedom, wisdom, and understanding. Your children should benefit from and share in your spiritual heritage.

A popular worldly view says, "I must stand aside and let my children develop in their own ways. They must *decide* their sexuality, they should be free to decide what church they attend or whether they will attend church at all, and they must grow up doing what they think is right, and I must support their choices."

If you think this hands-off view of parenting is exaggerated, watch your nightly newscast. Some parents have taken this idea to such extremes that they raise their children as "gender neutrals."[3] Even some committed Christians have thrown up their hands and resigned themselves to their kids' rebellion. OK. I get how hard parenting is, but are we really willing to stand by as our children suffer the terrible consequences of Satan's domination?

Let me say that if your children are adults, they are free, for better or worse, to make bad decisions. But as long as they are in your care and in your house, *you* are called to guide them. Parents are not called to cede their authority or surrender their children to darkness. Even if your children are grown, you can pray for their hearts to be softened by God's love.

So why do even Christian parents give up on multigenerational blessing and surrender their positions of authority in the family? I believe there are two basic reasons:

1. They do not yet know who *they* are and find themselves at a loss to give to their children what they themselves do not "own."

2. They focus on their own flaws and failures (their "Jacob*ness*") rather than the new creation (their "Israel*ness*"). Therefore, they pass on the sin mentality rather than the grace

> and blessing that flow through the DNA of the new birth.

Our families' generational destinies are literally in our hands. In my family tree, my father broke the curse and transformed our bloodline. As a result, he was able to pass his spiritual DNA on to me, and now Gayla and I have done the same for our children.

The rewards for staying the course are great. A pastor friend once told me, "Your sons are like racehorses." So I asked him what he meant by that. He explained, "They were bred to do what they do. They just can't help themselves. They were created to lead worship. They were created to preach and to move in the gifts. Your sons were created to heal the sick and speak prophetically. They were created to be leaders."

I had never thought of the racehorse analogy before, but he was absolutely right. Intentionality is key; the transfer of blessing from one generation to the next either happens by design or not at all. Even though someone broke the curse in my family line, Gayla and I cannot coast where the continuation of the blessing is concerned. We are still plowing the prophetic path for the generations yet to come.

The transfer of blessing is not a passive process. Gayla and I are committed to our active role. We use our authority and prophetic mandate to its fullest extent. We don't want any Rehoboams wreaking havoc in our future generations.

The Power of Heritage

We have talked a little about Paul and his protégé Timothy. Paul admonished Timothy to guard his spiritual heritage, both as it was received from his spiritual fathers and from his own bloodline. He said:

> *I remember you in my prayers night and day, greatly desiring to see you, being mindful of your tears, that I may be filled with joy, when I call to remembrance the genuine faith that is in you, which dwelt first in your grandmother Lois and your mother Eunice, and I am persuaded is in you also. Therefore I remind you to stir up the gift of God which is in you through the laying on of my hands* (2 Timothy 1:3-6).

Timothy was the product of multigenerational faith and blessing. His spiritual genetics were evident to Paul, who understood their power. Before his conversion, Paul was a Pharisee and the son of a Pharisee (see Acts 23:6). His Pharisaic roots played out powerfully in his deadly resistance to Christ and His followers.

Timothy did not ask for his heritage, and neither did we. Our skin and eye color, our musical abilities, our bone structure—all these came wrapped in our DNA. It was not my choice to have brown eyes, but Mama had brown eyes. I did not ask to be just under 6 feet tall, but I am. I might have preferred Daddy's 6' 5" frame, but that is not what my DNA programmed.

Our spiritual DNA is more powerful than the physical kind. Although it might not change your eye color or height, your spirit is designed to override your physical nature, just as Israel took ascendancy over Jacob. But spiritual DNA must be embraced in order to be fully manifested in our lives. It must also be acted upon and guarded for the transfer of blessing to be complete.

Spiritual Heritage Is a Two-Way Street

Do you remember when the mantle was transferred from Elijah to Elisha? Elijah asked his protégé what he wanted, and Elisha said, *"Please let a double portion of your spirit be upon me"* (2 Kings 2:9).

Elisha desired more of the blessing than his predecessor enjoyed. Elijah said, "That's a tough one, but if you'll stay focused on what is about to happen—and *only* if you stay focused—you'll have your double portion" (see 2 Kings 2:10).

From that point on, Elisha never took his eyes off Elijah. When the whirlwind swept the elder man up and away, the younger saw it and cried out, *"My father, my father"* (2 Kings 2:12).

The sons of the prophets who also served Elijah used the word *master* when referring to him (see 2 Kings 2:3,5). But Elisha called him *father.* This is very significant. You can have a meaningful relationship with your master, but he cannot give you his DNA—only a father can do that.

Elisha knew that his blessing originated with Elijah. Although his natural father could pass on his biological traits and his wealth, only Elijah could transfer what Elisha wanted most: the double portion anointing. Elisha was willing to pay whatever price was necessary to receive it.

Elisha was committed to the generational transfer. The spirit of Elijah ultimately rested on him *because* he recognized the elder man as his spiritual father. Therefore, when Elijah was gone, his DNA lived on.

The transfer "process" actually began when Elisha met his mentor. That is when his prophetic calling was activated. What he received was different from anything he'd ever known before or would ever experience again. It was a new realm of blessing, one which he would not relinquish even when his spiritual father was taken from him.

Elisha embraced the multigenerational blessing and anointing. He guarded it when he retrieved the mantle that fell from Elijah's shoulders. God's prophetic generation must guard the mantle of its forbears too. We do this by first valuing our spiritual parents, just as Elisha did.

This trait, however, is not typical of modern culture. Many (especially the young) would prefer to make their own way. It is common to reject the paths plowed by others because they are unoriginal. Often, the goal is to escape accountability. Either way, rejecting spiritual parenting leaves us unprepared for destiny fulfillment. Until we honor those who have gone before us, we will find it difficult to live in the blessing God has prepared for us.

Balancing the Old and New

There is a balance in honoring those who have gone before us without ritualizing our reverence. To be modern-day Elishas in the transfer of generational blessing, we must give honor where it is due but refuse to be bound by the traditions of men. If we will live by the Spirit, we will know when to submit and when to lead. We will understand the delicate balance between what God has said and done in the past and the new things that He will say and do in the future.

Our society places a premium on new things. People line up overnight for the privilege of dropping hundreds of dollars on a new iPhone or video game. Many are quick to embrace new perspectives on sexuality, marriage, and the unborn. Even new spouses are coveted by those who become bored with their "old" ones.

In the Church, many people run from meeting to meeting chasing after "new words." They like the emotional charge new prophecies ignite. This is an unbalanced approach, however. Isaiah 42:9 says: *"Behold, the former things have come to pass, and new things I declare; before they spring forth I tell you of them."*

The coming to pass of the former things precedes His declaring the new things. When God speaks, we must patiently await the fulfillment. But it is important to understand that this does not mean that God cannot speak until the last thing He said has been fulfilled. My point is that if we are so titillated by a new word that we discard the old, we will scuttle God's promises and compromise our own destinies.

To ensure the transference of the blessing, we must guard what God has already spoken. So, on the one hand, we must be patient; but on the other, we must know when to move on. Isaiah also wrote: *"Do not remember the former things, nor consider the things of old. Behold, I will do a new thing, now it shall spring forth; shall you not know it? I will even make a road in the wilderness and rivers in the desert"* (Isa. 43:18-19).

The Holy Spirit will guide us in the balance between the old and the new. Day by day, He will show us how to steward the blessing, embrace our heritage, and transfer it to our heirs. We have a mandate to be and to perpetuate God's prophetic generation. It is His plan, and by His grace we will fulfill it.

Think on This

What spiritual heritage have you received, and from whom? How are you a conduit? A container? What physical proof do you have of God's blessing/promise in your life? What gaps in the proof are discouraging? What demonic schemes have succeeded in interrupting the blessing in your bloodline? How are you actively working to receive the blessing from your predecessors and transfer it forward? How well are you balancing old and new? Explain.

Notes

1. Biblesoft's *New Exhaustive Strong's Numbers and Concordance with Expanded Greek-Hebrew Dictionary,* CD-ROM, Biblesoft, Inc. and International Bible Translators, Inc. (1994, 2003, 2006) s.v. "Ya`aqob," (OT3290).
2. *Blue Letter Bible,* Dictionary and Word Search for *"Yisra'el"* (Strong's 3478), 1996-2012, http://www.blueletterbible.org/lang/lexicon/lexicon.cfm?Strongs=H3478&t=KJV (accessed February 14, 2012).
3. David Wilkes, "Boy or girl? The parents who refused to say for FIVE years finally reveal sex of their 'gender-neutral' child," *Mail Online,* January 20, 2012, http://www.dailymail.co.uk/news/article-2089474/Beck-Laxton-Kieran-Cooper-reveal-sex-gender-neutral-child-Sasha.html (accessed February 3, 2012).

Chapter 10

Perpetuating Prophetic Legacy

Posterity will serve Him; future generations will be told about the Lord. They will proclaim His righteousness to a people yet unborn—for He has done it (Psalm 22:30-31 NIV).

In the messianic 22nd Psalm, David prophesied our role in proclaiming Christ's righteousness to future generations. David and others foretold our King's advent—an entire prophetic generation will declare His return. This mighty generation will witness what no one has seen in all of time. They will do more than sprinkle the world with His truth. Instead, their mouths will overflow with it.

The voices of God's prophetic generation might not come from the expected quarters. Yet they *will* come as bearers and perpetuators of our prophetic legacy, carriers of the DNA released into the Church 2,000 years ago. Only a prophetic

Church can transmit all that Joel prophesied. Only an army of mantle-passers can activate future generations. They must be warriors—the Abrahams, Elijahs, and Eunices of our day. We must adopt their mindsets as prophetic carriers who will not allow the promise to die in our Isaacs, our Elishas, or our Timothys.

We must have, on the one side of our legacy, devoted spiritual fathers and mothers who are committed to protecting and passing on their heritage. On the other side, we must have receivers who, like Elisha, refuse to take their eyes off it.

Prophetic Antitoxin: A Sure Word

Our prophetic legacy is not nourished in a vacuum; it must survive the foul climate of perversity. The corruption around us testifies to centuries of neglect, even in the Church. We have tried unsuccessfully to function without the sure word of prophecy that shines in a dark place (see 2 Pet. 1:19).

The sure word is the cure for oppression. Only a genuine *God said* can guide us past the world's sickness. It alone can save a teen from suicide and the unborn from the abortionist's mission. Only a *God said* can stem the tide of divorce and rebellion. A resounding "Thus saith the Lord" must be heard in the house of God and in the streets! It must be proclaimed, not by one voice or a handful of voices, but by an entire generation.

A sure word of prophecy will thwart the enemy's attack against young believers. It will set right those whom he has assaulted with confusion and religious substitutes. The voice of the living God will vanquish religious chaos. The authority in His voice will set in divine order everything that demonic entities have turned inside out. It will destroy the spirit of the devourer and every yoke of destruction, and it will proclaim restoration, even to the depths of darkness.

The man who prophesied the outpouring of the Holy Spirit on God's prophetic Church also proclaimed the day of restoration that would precede the return of our Lord:

> *And the floors shall be full of wheat, and the fats shall overflow with wine and oil. And I will restore to you the years that the locust hath eaten, the cankerworm, and the caterpiller, and the palmerworm, My great army which I sent among you. And ye shall eat in plenty, and be satisfied, and praise the name of the Lord your God, that hath dealt wondrously with you: and My people shall never be ashamed* (Joel 2:24-26 KJV).

The prophetic generation that ushers in the return of the Lord is a people refreshed and overflowing with wine and oil! Peter concurred with Joel, declaring Jesus's return after the promised restoration:

> *Repent therefore and be converted, that your sins may be blotted out, so that times of refreshing may come from the presence of the Lord, and that He may send Jesus Christ, who was preached to you before,* ***whom heaven must receive until the times of restoration of all things,*** *which God has spoken by the mouth of all His holy prophets since the world began* (Acts 3:19-21).

The prophetic generation is a life-speaking generation. They are people who separate themselves from those who curse the world. Instead, they are a curse-breaking, yoke-destroying generation ordained to deliver a sure word of prophecy. Their voices are creative; their words turn drought into overflow and the void into of a place of abundance.

The prophetic generation is not money-centric. Yet His Word and proven prophets have proclaimed that God will break the curse of lack among His people and return the world's wealth into their hands (see Prov. 13:22). Everything that has been devoured will be restored! The prophetic generation is being positioned to prosper so that the world may be prospered through them. God's people will take His sure word of prophecy to the corners of the globe—and then He will come again.

The authority in God's voice will set in divine order everything that demonic entities have turned inside out.

Legacy Dynamics

In Elijah's day, the sons of the prophets at Bethel and Jericho saw his departure coming and asked Elisha whether he did too: *"Do you know that the Lord will take away your master from over you today?"* (2 Kings 2:3,5).

Elisha did. As we have learned, he understood Elijah's critical role as a spiritual father and was not eager to lose him. Elisha valued the structure of authority that Elijah provided and drew strength from the spiritual atmosphere that Elijah's maturity engendered. Elisha craved that maturity for himself.

Spiritual fathers and mothers breed vitality into the generations that follow them; the prophetic generation must receive it. They must long for the guidance and correction their Elijahs will provide. They must soak in the anointing that is undergirded by their elders' spiritual authority. A truly prophetic generation is one that invites its predecessors to speak into their lives a deposit that leads them toward their destinies in God.

The authority of spiritual parents is not a light thing. Not everyone walks in the legitimate authority to speak into every other life. My sons walk in the generational blessing and anointing imprinted on the spiritual DNA of our family. Their legacy line is clear, but it is not necessarily exclusive. If, for example, one of my boys served under Bishop T.D. Jakes, then Brother Jakes would be authorized to make a spiritual deposit in my son's life as God directs.

But if a neighbor whom my son barely knows leaned over the fence and said, "I want to impart to your son what I have," I would tell him, "You may have spiritual authority over your sons, but have none where my boys are concerned."

Spiritual parent-child relationships are strategic kingdom pairings. They are not based on likability, friendship, or popularity. They are divine arrangements designed to ensure that our Elijahs don't take their anointings to the grave. They are strategic relationships that ensure the passing of legacy to the Elishas of our world.

When Elisha requested the double portion, he declared his awareness of spiritual succession. In essence, he said, "Elijah, your position is about to be vacated, and I want to fill it." It was a bold statement, but it was *exactly* what God had in mind. Elisha was the man God had chosen to take up the mantle.

I imagine Elijah's thoughts were like those of any serious spiritual parent who is closer to life's end than its beginning. They were probably similar to what I am thinking in the second half of my life: *I am determined not to take the anointing to the grave. It is up to me to extend the legacy by fighting for its preservation and its transference to every one of my spiritual (and natural) sons and daughters. What I've seen in my dad's life, and now in my own, must be carried into the next generation and however many generations there will be before Jesus comes again.*

Do you remember how Joseph carried his promise and the thread of his father's prophetic legacy through his difficult life in Egypt? Consider the opposition he faced—what a testament to his tenacity and conviction! I believe a modern "Joseph generation" will push past the curse that distorts modern times and steward a legacy so powerful that the landscape of the world will be transformed!

The word translated *master* in Second Kings 2:3 and 2:5 is *adon,* which means "lord, master, owner."[1] It is the root from which we get *Adonai,* the name of God that reveals our position as His servants. The prophetic generation values its predecessors and its own role as sons, daughters, and servants.[2]

Two Steps Forward, None Back

The prophet Joel wrote: *"But Judah shall abide forever, and Jerusalem from generation to generation"* (Joel 3:20). Joel saw a legacy without end that would be preserved one generation at a time.

We have already seen the precarious state of the generational anointing: unless we are vigilant, it will soon be extinct. The spiritual legacy of God's prophetic Church was not intended to be interrupted, and certainly not extinguished. It is a precious commodity that was meant to be built upon, revelation by revelation, generation by generation, so that the next generation would always supersede the one before it.

Dominion is an essential part of building upon our spiritual and prophetic legacy (see Gen. 1:26). God entrusted us with dominion over the earth. Even Nebuchadnezzar recognized how God had ordained dominion to flow: *"How great are His signs, and how mighty His wonders! His kingdom is an everlasting kingdom, and* ***His dominion is from generation to generation"*** (Dan. 4:3).

If we walk in dominion, we will fulfill the potential of our spiritual authority. God's intent is that it would result in our children doing the same, but to an even greater degree than us. The same increase should be seen throughout our generations.

Let me warn you of the obvious: just because God intends for us to live a certain way does not guarantee that we will. You and I must rise up daily with a dominion mindset and an unrelenting dedication to preserving and transferring the legacy of a prophetic generation. We must keep ourselves stirred; we must remain spiritually active and vigilant to guard all that has been passed on to us.

To keep advancing, we must be a prophetic, stalwart, curse-breaking, yoke-destroying generation that guards our natural and supernatural bloodlines. It is incumbent upon us to understand the enemy's ways. He is not watching idly from the sidelines; he is actively trying to sever the legacy lifelines in our families and spheres of influence. His goal is to kill within our Isaacs that which the Abrahams imparted. If he fails to trip up the former, he will redouble his effort to send our Jacobs into a spiritual stall pattern.

We have a responsibility to protect our children from the devourer. It is time for us to leave the La-Z-Boy and consciously prepare them for legacy transfer. It is time we stopped dragging them and ourselves to church as though it were a lifeless, obligatory act. We need to quit showing up late and telegraphing to our kids that praise and worship aren't important. It is time to quit stroking their youthful rebellion and setting them up to have the legacy stolen from their very laps!

It is time we were the example. We need to show our children that worship is the epicenter of our lives and our walk with God. This is not the time to dawdle in the lobby, talking about our new snowblowers or our neighbors' business. It is up to us to model fresh passion for what is happening at God's house. When we set *our* priorities in order, our children's lives will be transformed.

My parents were vigilant. When I was an infant, my bassinet was on the front row of the church. In fact, I *grew up* on the front row. As a toddler, that's where my playpen was parked. When I was old enough, my parents planted my hindquarters on the front pew. I was there for every service.

This is what legacy transfer is all about. It is not a one-time event; it is not a ceremony in which your kids are zapped into spiritual gianthood. Legacy transfer is a day-to-day process that will set you on fire one day and your children on fire the next. Legacy is perishable and comes at a price. I am glad my parents were willing to pay it. They gave me a gift I can never repay, but am eager to pass on.

The gift "stuck." When I was old enough to attend Sunday school, I would sneak out to sit on the front row to hear my father preach. I wanted to witness the power and presence of God. I loved seeing people rise out of their wheelchairs. I got excited to see prayer change lives. I experienced the reality of His love and power firsthand. Because the legacy was passed on from my earliest days, I grew up longing for the things of God rather than the things of the world.

My spirit grieves because I see a generation that has never known such hunger. My heart breaks when I think that a generation as yet unborn could endure an even more lifeless experience. We have a responsibility to them! We must introduce them to our mighty God. We must share the knowledge of His might, power, Spirit, and Word. For the legacy to advance, we must help our generations to discover and build upon the revelation we have received. If we don't do it, who will? And what will be the outcome for our children?

It's Not About Us

Legacy is transferred by people who see beyond the boundaries of their own lives and needs. Spiritually speaking, legacy is prioritized by people who think, not in terms of maintenance, but in terms of increase. When we studied the characteristics of God's prophetic generation, we learned that they are a visionary people. They are determined to protect the territory they have won, but they are also determined to possess the ground of the future. Prophetic people are not plateau-dwellers; they reject comfort zones and survival mode. They have discarded the "us four and no more" mentality, and they always look outward.[3]

Whatever we do, it is up to us to get on board with God's kingdom vision. The Church has chased rabbit trails far too long. Too many ministries are more determined to fulfill their plans than to answer the desires of His heart. Because of their spiritual self-absorption, they lose sight of how their destinies fit into God's big picture.

He wants *all* of our destinies fulfilled. What He will not tolerate is for isolated atolls of anointing to reach pinnacles of success while they remain disconnected from His larger kingdom plan. I believe this flawed mentality is the reason so many ministries suffer lack. Why would God underwrite endeavors that are contrary to His will? Before we become frustrated with God's seeming failure to provide, we should ask ourselves, "Am I doing God's thing, or my own?"

The Church will always have leaders, but in the prophetic generation there are no pew warmers. We are called to be a people with a leadership mentality. That means we are required to embrace character development. He will not settle for church-sponsored comfort zones designed to harbor the spiritually lazy. The world is spiraling downward; we are called to lead them to Christ. Therefore, we need to be maturity-minded rather than comfort-driven.

Oral Roberts was a spiritual father to many. He loved people, but he did not coddle them. He was determined to transfer legacy, and that sometimes meant helping his spiritual sons and daughters to move their focus from self to kingdom. A very well-known minister once complained to Oral about the negative press he was receiving. The man was deeply hurt by insinuations that had been made, and felt that he was being treated unfairly.

Oral was not swayed by the man's suppositions. He rose above the level of emotion and sympathy and got to the nub of the issue. "Did you do the things they said you did?" he asked.

The man of God responded, "Well, yes."

"Did you spend ministry money on the things they accused you of spending it on?" he inquired further.

"Uh, yes, sir. I did."

"Then why are you crying? You did not manage your resources properly. You have not shown discretion in your decisions. Yet you want to cry because somebody wrote about it. If you don't want them to write about it, don't do it."

As an Elijah to the next generation and a man of integrity, Brother Roberts did not hesitate to correct a man of universal stature. He kept his eyes fixed on God's eternal plan and helped the man recognize that it is not about us.

The Stir of the New

Imagine living in Israel at the time of Christ. We often overlook the stir He created. The opening of blind eyes might seem like old news to us, but in Jesus's day it was unheard of. No one had ever seen such a thing. Jesus's ministry created controversy at every turn. His audacity to heal on the Sabbath, to speak of the forgiveness of sins, and to hang around with undesirables completely upended the status quo (see Luke 14:3-5; Matt. 9:2-5;10-13).

I believe God's prophetic generation is about to arise. They will create a stir, just as Jesus did. They will walk in a level of the supernatural that will challenge others and crash the philosophical grid. When the sick are raised from their hospital beds by the healing power of God, the world will notice. Not everyone will rejoice to see the captives set free. Not everybody rejoiced when Jesus set captives free!

God's prophetic generation must be prepared to weather the controversy and continue in their calling. They will embrace the stir of the supernatural and continue to walk in love toward their detractors. Even the naysayers who refuse salvation will be unable to deny the miracles. When they see limbs grow out and the insane made whole, they will have no choice but to bear witness to the supernatural power of God.

God has something powerful in His mouth for this season. His proceeding word will reveal the things that were seemingly hidden. For His prophetic generation, it will come as no surprise, because He has revealed His will for centuries. The world, however, will be skeptical. Isaiah describes these dichotomous reactions to the stir that is coming:

> *Long ago I told you what was going to happen. Then suddenly I took action, and all My predictions came true. For I know how stubborn and obstinate you are. Your necks are as unbending as iron. Your heads are as hard as bronze. That is why I told you what would happen; I told you beforehand what I was going to do. Then you could never say, "My idols did it. My wooden image and metal god commanded it to happen!"* (Isaiah 48:3-5 NLT)

And then he continues:

> *You have heard; see all this. And will you not declare it? I have made you hear new things from this time, even hidden things, and you did not know them. They are created now...* (Isaiah 48:6-7).

Hidden things are about to be uncovered—now. God's prophetic generation will be instrumental in the process, and you were created to be a part of it. It will not be a cakewalk; but it will be glorious. To handle it, the Church will need a strong diet of meat. The full Gospel must become real in our hearts and manifested in the earth.

I believe this is why prophetic voices have hammered home the messages of God's love and our identity in Christ over the course of recent decades. When Oral Roberts coined the phrase, "Something good is going to happen to you," he was not creating a motto to be remembered by. God gave those words to Oral Roberts so people's expectations would line up with His goodness.

Religion has declared for years: "You never know what God will do. Better watch out. He might just take you out." Christians *expected* bad things to happen. As a result, the Church became spiritually impotent. God gave Oral Roberts a single sentence with which to reverse the poisoned mindset of the Church—not just so they would feel better about life, but so that they could become the prophetic instrument He intended them to be.

That is why I continue to say, "You are who God says you are." For us to be His prophetic generation, to have His eternal perspective, and to be willing to lay down our lives for something that might be fulfilled after we leave this earth, we must believe it.

There must be a remnant equipped and willing to prioritize the Church's prophetic mandate on the basis of His proceeding word—a remnant unwilling to leave behind a powerless generation of those who heard of the anointing, but never witnessed it, who heard of His presence, but never experienced it, and whose forbears operated in the gifts, but took them to the grave for eternity.

If you have experienced even a moment of His glory, if you remember a day when your calling burned deep in your heart, if you are leading a congregation, or a family, or one hurting soul into the light, then you have a legacy which must be transferred—every day until you leave this earth and enter your eternal reward.

Think on This

Consider ways in which you can become a stronger, more determined "Abraham" in passing spiritual legacy to the "Isaacs" in your life. Why is an entire prophetic generation needed to usher in the return of Christ? What is your place of spiritual authority? Who are the Elishas in your midst? What impact are you having on them? How are you guarding the legacy lifeline? What is your response to the stir of the new?

Notes

1. Biblesoft's *New Exhaustive Strong's Numbers and Concordance with Expanded Greek-Hebrew Dictionary.* CD-ROM. Biblesoft, Inc. and International Bible

Translators, Inc. (© 1994, 2003, 2006) s.v. "adown" or "adon" (OT 113).

2. See Chapter 4.
3. Again, see Chapter 4 for more about this.

Chapter 11

His Glorious Church

Husbands, love your wives, just as Christ also loved the church and gave Himself for her, that He might sanctify and cleanse her with the washing of water by the word, that He might present her to Himself a glorious church, not having spot or wrinkle or any such thing, but that she should be holy and without blemish (Ephesians 5:25-27).

Jesus promised to come for His Church, the Bride for whom He gave the last precious drop of His blood. Before He carries her across heaven's threshold, His Bride will be made complete. Even now, she is being sanctified and washed in His Word, so that when she is presented to her Groom, she will be *glorious.*

This Bride's heritage cannot be separated from her future glory. Her DNA came from the Groom. She is "genetically" empowered to rise to her position of authority in the earth and speak in His name. She does this under His perfect headship, as it was ordained by the Father who *"put all things under* [Jesus Christ's] *feet, and gave Him to be head over all things to the church"* (Eph. 1:22).

The Church's multigenerational heritage is woven throughout Scripture. Wherever Christ is revealed, the Bride's bloodline is revealed as well. The first-century apostolic fathers were impassioned receivers of this divine legacy. They embraced their Messiah as the One who was promised. Therefore, they received His ministry mantle and transferred it to the next generation.

When Jesus said, *"You are Peter, and on this rock I will build My church, and the gates of Hades shall not prevail against it"* (Matt. 16:18), He signaled the handoff and the setting in motion of a generational process. When He said, *"Follow Me, and I will make you fishers of men"* (Matt. 4:19), He guided His progeny's steps into His genetic footprint. He extended His bloodline through a Body birthed to carry His message across the earth and through the centuries.

The Lord who nourishes and cherishes His Church (see Eph. 5:29) transferred a legacy that transformed His 12, ignited the 120, and changed the world from that day to this!

THE TRUE ORDINATION

From the Church's beginnings, men and women have been set apart, not by human consensus, but at the direction of the Holy Spirit. At Antioch, devotion to prayer and fasting, attention to the voice of the Spirit, and the laying on of hands led to the sending of Paul and Barnabas to the Gentiles:

> *Now in the church that was at Antioch there were certain prophets and teachers: Barnabas, Simeon who was called Niger, Lucius of Cyrene, Manaen who had been brought up with Herod the tetrarch, and Saul. As they ministered to the Lord and fasted, the Holy Spirit said, "Now separate to Me Barnabas and Saul for the work to which I have called them." Then, having fasted and prayed, and laid hands on them, they sent them away* (Acts 13:1-3).

A board vote and a certificate are not enough. The bloodline will not be extended by earthly methods. At the leadership level, the legacy of Christ is transferred through the prophetic, Spirit-led ordination of His messengers, not the filling out of applications and the casting of ballots. His prophetic, glorious Church cannot live on the bread of human ideas, but by every word that proceeds from the mouth of God (see Deut. 8:3).

What Church Is and Isn't

Why do we attend church? Why don't we just curl up in our pajamas, grab some coffee and an Internet connection, and let it go at that?

Before I ruffle any more feathers than necessary, let me explain. I understand the challenges faced by the bedridden, the incarcerated, and others who are physically unable to attend regular services. I assure you of this: God is faithful to meet us where we are and able to work in our lives whatever the circumstances.

For most of us, however, assembling together as the Body of Christ is a matter of choice—an important choice that millions of the most persecuted make, even when showing up *literally* means risking life and limb.

Why are the persecuted so intent on attendance? Because of what church *is.* The corporate worship service is a place where dry bones are restored to life and spiritual droughts are broken. It provides an environment conducive to maturation, one in which we are regularly reminded of who we are and where we are going. It is a hothouse of *God saids* that deliver us from the wilderness and into our promised land.

Church *is not* a spiritual gymnasium or lecture hall of higher biblical learning. Neither is it a spiritual drive-thru for those seeking an emotional buzz. Although corporate worship provides benefit in these areas, they are not at the heart of our gathering together. People do not occupy pews to display their spiritual strength or to simply learn the meanings of Greek words. And, even though most people find comfort in church, that is not the only reason we gather.

The Church was designed as a place of spiritual activation and a force against which the gates of hell would not prevail (see Matt. 16:18). It should be a place where assignments are clarified, gifts are honed, and troops are equipped for battle. It is a center of individual and corporate transformation. If that is not what church is for us, then where did the original DNA of the prophetic Church go?

As God's prophetic instrument, the Church should drive culture, not react or succumb to it. The Church is *the* conduit of prophetic power, a divine plumb line in the midst of our warped generation. Each congregation either stands as a beacon of truth or becomes enmeshed in (and subject to) the world's system.

Authenticity and Timing

If ever there was an appropriate time for religious clubs or the CEO concept of church, I can assure you it has ended. The Church was not created to be powerless. The Church was birthed to unleash the power of the Spirit throughout our world. It succeeds in its calling to the extent that the Holy Spirit is allowed to flow in and through each of us.

Jesus is our ultimate example of divine power operating on the human plane. He decreed the passing of His mantle when He commissioned us with these words:

> *And these signs will follow those who believe: In My name they will cast out demons; they will speak with new tongues; they will take up serpents; and if they drink anything deadly, it will by no means hurt them; they will lay hands on the sick, and they will recover* (Mark 16:17-18).

These signs are heaven's stamp of authenticity. Their release surges as the apostolic and prophetic foundation of the Church is restored (see Eph. 2:20). This is how the Church possesses the land: it does the things that can only be accomplished by the Spirit of the living God!

It is not about one man or one woman or one affiliation or denomination. It is about apostles raising up and leading the next generation of apostolic leaders, and about prophets speaking under the true unction of the Spirit in order to provide direction and insight into hidden things. It is about evangelists, pastors, and teachers expanding the kingdom, maturing the ranks, and preparing their successors to carry the torch forward.

God's prophetic Church must precede the Second Coming of Christ. John the Baptist prepared his generation for the entrance of Messiah, but a prophetic Body will herald His return. The unmistakable voice of God's prophetic army will cry aloud in our modern wilderness: "Prepare the way of the Lord!"

Timing is essential. *His* timing will shatter our "holy myths" about the date of Christ's return. Most of us see that day as having been circled in red on heaven's calendar. But I believe the timing is linked, not to a date, but to a condition—the readiness of the Church. Time clocks are not the issue; He is not coming for an almost-glorious Church. He is coming for an unblemished Bride.

It takes a prophetic generation to prepare the Bride and the world for Christ's return. Only a prophetic Church—the one unveiled on the Day of Pentecost—can become His glorious Church. It was birthed in the prophetic and its glory will be activated in the prophetic. The voice of His prophetic generation will ready the Church and pave the way; they will be instrumental in the unfolding of events that must precede His return.

This is not a book about eschatology; it is about the prophetic. My point is that timing works God's way and not ours, as the Exodus from Egypt reveals. God led His people out on a journey that, logically speaking, would be brief. Instead, days became decades, not because God's GPS was on the fritz, but because His timing was linked to the condition of His people.

The Israelites were out of Egypt, but Egypt was not yet out of them. God never balked at the four-decade delay. He was willing to forego the swift fulfillment of the promise. His timing was predicated on having a people who were ready for their role. He would not give the Promised Land to a fearful bunch who cowered at the sight of giants He'd already promised to deal with (see Num. 13–14). Instead, God waited until the Israelites' maturation was sufficient for them to create the circumstances for their conquest.

The Father is not fixed to our concepts of time. He will not send Christ into the flailing arms of a dilapidated Bride—His Son will be received by a Bride suitable for the King. He will return when she is ready and has readied the world.

The Body of Truth

When the disciples asked Jesus about the signs of His coming and the end of the age, He gave them guidelines by which to distinguish deceptions from legitimate signals (see Matt. 24:3-14). He then laid down a bright line of demarcation, saying, *"And this gospel of the kingdom will be preached in all the world as a witness to all the nations, and then the end will come"* (Matt. 24:14).

The Gospel of the kingdom was not Jesus's reference to user-friendly adaptations of Scripture. He referred to *His* Gospel; it is the full Gospel that reveals His way of doing and being. Clever attempts at inclusive, watered-down, common-denominator "gospels" will not pass His muster. His Gospel is like Him—*unchanging.* He and it will stand when all else has fallen.

The Gospel is the Church's mandate in the earth. Notice how Paul stressed her essential role in a letter to Timothy:

> *These things I write to you, though I hope to come to you shortly; but if I am delayed, I write so that*

> *you may know how you ought to conduct yourself in the house of God, which is* ***the church of the living God, the pillar and ground of the truth*** (1 Timothy 3:14-15).

The Gospel guides the conduct of the Church, which, in turn, serves as *"the pillar and ground of the truth."* The Church must rest on the full Gospel if she is to stake the world to God's truth. A redacted "gospel" is unacceptable. Vain philosophies will not do. A scrubbed "gospel" devoid of the blood and the cross has no power. It is our job to preach *the* Gospel. An intellectual "gospel" cannot save. The true Gospel was not intended to appeal to logic. His truth can be received only by faith. Any "gospel" that is tailored to satisfy the senses is a deception. It is a form of witchcraft dressed in religious robes.

The Gospel taxes the natural mind. It does not exist to be completely understood by the intellect; it is to be believed by the heart. Philosophies stroke the intellect—they boast not of God, but of human ability. Ephesians 2:8-9 teaches the opposite message: *"For by grace you have been saved through faith, and that not of yourselves; it is the gift of God, not of works, lest anyone should boast."* His is the Gospel of grace. It does not stroke the egos of the strong; it empowers God's people to do what human strength and ability are incapable of doing. It is not a religious word, but the literal word of life.

Remember where our discussion of the prophetic began:

> *So He humbled you, allowed you to hunger, and fed you with manna which you did not know nor did your fathers know, that He might make you*

> *know that* ***man shall not live by bread alone; but man lives by every word that proceeds from the mouth of the Lord*** (Deuteronomy 8:3).

When you have the word of life, you have a promise straight from the mouth of God. His proceeding word creates order out of chaos, light out of darkness, and abundance out of drought. His word empowers His people.

Nevertheless, the Gospel also offends. Paul explained that *"the message of the cross is foolishness to those who are perishing, but to us who are being saved it is the power of God. For it is written: 'I will destroy the wisdom of the wise, and bring to nothing the understanding of the prudent'"* (1 Cor. 1:18-19).

No wonder the Gospel offends people! The so-called wise do not want their wisdom proven wrong. We humans dislike having our assumptions challenged. Accepting the Gospel on its terms means tearing down the structures we have spent our whole lives building. It means recanting the very beliefs we have espoused as truth.

The Gospel *should* be a stumbling block. The sheer power of truth should challenge intellects and bring conviction. The truth we are commissioned to uphold must not be edited. There *is* a hell. The lost *will* suffer eternal agonies. So-called "gospels" of syncretism and inclusion are nothing more than spiritual casseroles of New Age layered with hints of truth to make them palatable. These deceptions will cause millions or even billions to perish.

The blood must be preached. Without the blood, there is no Gospel and we are left to our own insufficient devices. We might dedicate ourselves and our pulpits to appearances of unity, but unless we uphold scriptural integrity, desecration will be the real result. Warmed over, adulterated sermons might satisfy the appetites of the spiritually shallow, but they will poison the bloodstream and prevent restoration. Unless the sacrifice of the cross and the power of the blood bind our central message, we will become Satan's best accomplices in his quest to destroy lives and nations.

When you preach the uncompromised Gospel of the kingdom, truth takes the witness stand and proves its own fulfillment. Instead of mere talk of healing, the message will produce its own verification. And instead of another conversation about restoration, the message will release the very manifestation of restoration. Only the uncompromised Gospel can speak and create. Only His Word can promise transformation and produce transformed lives.

When the truth—the Gospel of the kingdom—is preached, signs and wonders will follow: The dead will be raised. The bound will be delivered. Our children will flock to church, hungry for God's presence. Neighbors will see God's goodness in our lives and fall to their knees before Him. Families will be made whole and will become the sanctuaries He designed them to be.

When the Body of Christ settles for nothing less than the whole truth, the Church and the world will be readied for His return.

Instrument of Dominion

From beginning to end, the Gospel reveals our dominion in the earth. God instructed Adam from the outset, saying, *"Be fruitful and multiply; fill the earth and subdue it;* ***have dominion*** *over the fish of the sea, over the birds of the air, and over every living thing that moves on the earth"* (Gen. 1:28).

God's people are His agents in the earth. We are supposed to exercise dominion, just as Adam and Eve did at the beginning. Their dominion was not designed to be forfeited. It was intended to be transferred from generation to generation, as we have already seen in the Book of Daniel, which states: *"How great are His signs, and how mighty His wonders! His kingdom is an everlasting kingdom, and His dominion is from generation to generation"* (Dan. 4:3).

The Church is not just a gathering place; it is a proponent of God's dominion. This idea rubs against the grain of modern mindsets that prize false humility and other distortions of truth. As with every other element of His will, dominion cannot be understood or transferred unless the full Gospel is preached.

How can we ignore the call to dominion when Paul expressed God's will for the Church so clearly in his Spirit-inspired letter to the Ephesians?

> *To me, who am less than the least of all the saints, this grace was given, that I should preach among the Gentiles the unsearchable riches of Christ, to make all see what is the fellowship of the mystery, which from the beginning of the ages has been hidden in God who created all things through Jesus Christ; to the intent that* ***now the manifold wisdom of God might be made known by the church to the principalities and powers in the heavenly places, according to the eternal***

> ***purpose which He accomplished in Christ Jesus our Lord*** (Ephesians 3:8-11).

God appointed His prophetic army to bring His power and authority to bear on demonic forces, wherever they are found! We are to exercise our dominion—to occupy—every system, organization, nation, and continent by operating in His authority until He comes (see Luke 19:13 KJV).

VISION OF AN INGLORIOUS CHURCH

Jesus is coming for a glorious Church. His will shall be done. I am determined to see that day, but whether it happens in my lifetime or not, I will hold His vision in my heart; I will work toward its fulfillment and proclaim it until I draw my last breath.

Although I have not minced words in exposing chinks in the Church's armor, my purpose has never been to magnify shortcomings. My mission is to keep God's vision before His people, as the prophet Habakkuk was told to do:

> *Then the Lord answered me and said: "Write the vision and make it plain on tablets, that he may run who reads it. For the vision is yet for an appointed time; but at the end it will speak, and it will not lie. Though it tarries, wait for it; because it will surely come, it will not tarry"* (Habakkuk 2:2-3).

The way of the earth is compromise and decay. Unless we are vigilant, we will settle for religious facsimiles without even realizing it. When I was just 19 years old, God gave me a vision of this spiritual decay. I was scheduled to preach a one-week revival in Winnipeg, Canada. The auditorium seated several hundred and was crammed full each night. As the weeks wore on and the power of God was manifested, crowds were drawn to the point that people gathered outside and peered into the windows. All kinds of people came, including biker gangs and other subculture groups. Across the board, they got saved, filled with the Spirit, and delivered.

After preaching nightly for almost four weeks, I lay across my bed one afternoon for a nap. I was conscious and aware of my surroundings, but entered what seemed like a quasi-sleep state. The Lord took me by the hand and showed me a ritzy neighborhood in which a magnificent cathedral was surrounded by multimillion-dollar homes.

He took me into the mansions' kitchens, all of which were staffed by servants. The pantries and refrigerators were well stocked with the very best provisions. Yet, when He led me inside the cathedral, I saw a people suffering from starvation. They were emaciated and literally reduced to skin and bones—their stomachs were bloated and they were desperate for any morsel of food they could find.

In the pulpit was the man of God dressed in regal robes and holding a cup of birdseed. Every so often, he would pinch a few seeds between his thumb and forefinger and flick them toward the congregation. Once, as the seeds landed, a woman wearing a full-length mink coat and a ten-carat diamond ring lunged to the floor to claim and devour the seed. She was so emaciated that her enormous ring spun around her finger as she groveled. At the height of the vision, God said, "It is for this cause that I have raised you up—to feed My sheep!"

This is what motivates me. This is the reason I am willing to cry aloud, spare not, and lift my voice as a trumpet in the midst of this generation (see Isa. 58:1). In too many quarters, pastors and other leaders are dispensing meager portions to the spiritually starving. They toss a seed here and a seed there when meat is what is needed—*and lots of meat.*

How can we address the world's famines while spiritual famine plagues the house of God? How can we take dominion of the earth when malnourishment robs the Church of its desire to change the world? *It is time for the glorious Church to emerge.* It is time for the Bride to prepare for her Groom and do His bidding.

> *"A posterity shall serve Him. It will be recounted of the Lord to the next generation, they will come and declare His righteousness to a people who will be born..."* (Psalm 22:30-31).

Profile of His Glorious Church

The glorious Church of Jesus Christ will cast a large, indelible footprint on our planet and in the heavenlies. She will be a pulsating force, not of human nature, but of the divine nature. The Bride will reflect Jesus in every way: She will be house of plenty, able to nourish and replenish people and communities, regions, and nations. She will be irresistibly magnetic, as He is, attracting people to Christ from the far corners of the globe and restoring them and their communities to wholeness.

David saw such a day and prophesied about it, writing:

> *All the ends of the world shall remember and turn to the Lord, and all the families of the nations shall worship before You. For the kingdom is the Lord's, and He rules over the nations* (Psalm 22:27-28).

The glorious Church will precisely reflect His kingdom. His glory will be seen, not by a few, but by the masses. She will shake the world from its slumber and reveal the cracks in its foundation. She will stoke the hunger of her own and of the unchurched. She will be filled with those who yearn for more of Him. These are the high-place people David described centuries ago:

> *Who may ascend into the hill of the Lord? Or who may stand in His holy place? He who has clean hands and a pure heart, who has not lifted up his soul to an idol, nor sworn deceitfully. He shall receive blessing from the Lord, and righteousness from the God of his salvation. This is Jacob, the generation of those who seek Him, who seek Your face. Selah* (Psalm 24:3-6).

His glorious Church will produce a pure-hearted people willing to pay the price of His glory. They will seek the high spiritual ground where His *shekinah* glory rests. They will not be a perfect people, but a perfected Church of those who have put themselves in His care and wrapped themselves in His grace. Their lives will testify that *"God is with the generation of the righteous"* (Ps. 14:5).

Just as His kingdom knows no lack, the glorious Church will not experience poverty. Because the kingdom is replete with His power, the glorious Church will be powerful. Because He said she would be without spot, wrinkle, or blemish (see Eph. 5:27), His glorious Church will be free of perversion, bigotry, defilement, and any other blot inflicted to destroy and condemn.

His glorious Church will be an undistorted conduit for His Word. The Gospel will be proclaimed in all truth and power, and it will pierce *"even to the division of soul and spirit, and of joints and marrow"* (Heb. 4:12). His Word will release the full force of His *dunamis* power to produce a wonder-working Church. *"The people who know their God shall be strong, and carry out great exploits"* (Dan. 11:32).

This will not be a needy Church, but a Body able to disperse to others His goodness, grace, mercy, truth, and provision. It will be a place where relationships are restored, marriages are nourished, and children are raised, knowing from the earliest ages that they are who God says they are.

Hopelessness will not be found in His glorious Church. It will be the very hub of hope, a center of transformation, and an environment in which 120 can change the world in mere moments. Its pews will be filled, but that will not be the Church's purpose. It will once again form the spiritual bedrock of every community and be a company so aligned with God's standards that the culture of the world can no longer dictate to her. Instead, society will bow its knee to the Most High God.

His glorious Church is not toothless or downcast. She is not poor or prejudiced. She is not marked by immorality, complacency, or any other condition that defies the kingdom model. His glorious Church is an assembly of new creations unified in His love to manifest His power, will, and nature throughout the earth.

It will take a prophetic generation to become such a Church. That is the generation that will make the way for the return of our Lord Jesus Christ!

HIGHER WAYS

God's idea of a glorious Church is the gold standard. He will not settle for an approximation. God never lowers His expectations to accommodate ours (see Isa. 55:8-9).

In our humanity, His perfection is unattainable. Yet, even in our frailties and carnality, He is empowering us to rise up to our appointed stature. In His name and by His Spirit, we will bind the enemy under our feet and be the Church He desires. This is His plan and He ordained us to be part of it.

CONDITIONED FOR GLORY

Glimpses of His glorious Church are appearing worldwide. In pockets of the United States, churches are throwing off pretense and religious yokes. They are getting on their knees and getting their hands dirty. They have made up their minds that they were created for authentic moves of God, however messy they might be.

Internationally, the Church is transforming some of the most unlikely regions into bastions of His unmitigated power. In places where a watered-down Gospel would save face and avoid trouble, the truth is brought forth in power. The cross and the blood of Christ are not set aside, but lifted up! Witchcraft is being challenged and small groups of servant-minded believers are revolutionizing their cities.

I am convinced that revival is coming and will eclipse any revival in Church history. Imagine a move of God that makes Azusa Street look like Sunday school class! The coming revival will reveal the weight of His glory to a degree not yet witnessed. Resurrections and creative miracles will erupt like never before. Men and women of God will prophesy—their words will shake environments and bring rapid, mind-boggling manifestations. Signs and wonders will be seen in the open by large numbers of people. The airwaves will be filled, not with pornography and licentiousness, but with divine acts able to make the whole earth tremble.

It will not be an easy season. It is hard to imagine how it could be. The world's deteriorating condition tells us that satanic forces have pulled out the stops. Simultaneously, God is shaking everything that can be shaken, including the demonic kingdom. He is rallying His people to come out from under the world's system and line up with His priorities.

Calamity may very well stir this revival. The breaking down of society as we know it is already shaking the world out of its stupor and bringing the Church to her feet. Events, for better or worse, are playing out in the extreme. Battle lines are clearly drawn. The enemy's strategies are eye-popping; nevertheless, when God moves, no one will doubt that it is Him.

The coming revival will force people to the point of decision. They will be compelled to move forward with God or break with Him forever. In the United States, I believe signs and wonders will restore the nation. We have allowed the enemy to ravage our country and our values. While we can and should make our voices heard, we will not take back our nation by political means. No president, Supreme Court, or any Congress will save us—only God.

Only God can snap the resistance of stiff necks; only He can soften hardened hearts. I believe the coming move of God will bend the knees of the Pharaohs and Ninevehs of this world and reveal to them the living God who cannot be defeated or appeased.

This will be a season of increased prophetic clarity that will open doors to earthly thrones and other seats of power. The Church will gain greater access to secular authorities and they will hear the prophets speak of what is coming. Whether or not they are humble enough to heed God's messengers, they, and the entire world, will see their prophecies fulfilled. The mass media outlets that have brazenly defied God will have no choice but to display His power as events unfold.

Day by day and revelation by revelation, we are being conditioned to manifest His glorious Church. Remember that we are the earthly mechanism that restrains the works of the enemy (see 2 Thess. 2:1-8). When we are gone, Satan will run roughshod over the earth. Those who bemoaned the "constraints" of Christianity will beg for the Church to return.

They will awaken too late. The salt and light that is the Body of Christ will be raptured before the earth's darkest days begin. Meanwhile, we are being groomed to step into the fullness of our God-given power and authority. Our wrinkles, spots, and blemishes must be dealt with before we can complete our work and be translated from the earth. By the time He comes for us, we will look much different than we do now. We will be a force to be reckoned with, far better able to restrain the works of darkness than we are now.

THE RAPTURE-READY, GLORIOUS CHURCH

Many Christians see the Rapture as a day on which God will flip the switch on His divine-strength Dyson and vacuum His people up from the earth and into glory. This is a distortion of the truth; the Rapture is the translation of the Church. Like Enoch, those believers who are alive on the earth will walk with God and leave this world without dying. Instead, we will be translated, as Enoch and Elijah were (see Gen. 5:24; 2 Kings 2:11).

The Church must be raptured prior to the Tribulation. The restraint she provides against the *"son of perdition"* (2 Thess. 2:3) must be removed for the Tribulation to occur. Second Thessalonians 2:1-8 clearly shows that the restraining force of the Church will be removed before the Antichrist openly takes his place in end-times events.

His glorious Church will walk with God and not die. She will reign with such power and authority as to activate the transition from the season of restraint to that of the great and terrible Tribulation.

Conclusion

From the loins of God's prophetic generation will come His glorious Church. They will be His warriors and heralds preparing a dying world for the return of Christ. In the midst of an evil and adulterous generation, they will be trained to fulfill the conditions necessary for God to unleash the end of days.

This generation has begun forming. I see them in the pews of our church and in pews around the world. Week after week, they press into God and against spiritual wickedness. They hunger and thirst for righteousness and are filled (see Matt. 5:6). They train up their children and transfer the anointing and blessing from generation to generation. They are like the 120 who changed the earth 2,000 years ago—spiritual movers and shakers willing to lay down everything the world offers because they value His glory above all earthly treasures.

This is a generation of those who stand strong in a dark age. They know who they are and are unwilling to operate beneath the level of their privileges or prophetic birthright. They *refuse* to live beneath the level of what God can do and give. They are the Church that God will translate to heaven.

But first, they will be propelled north, south, east, and west with the proceeding word that declares and creates life. This prophetic generation will not be silenced. They are native speakers in the tongues of God. They operate in His anointing and respond in faith. They are possessors of the promised territory, and they do not fear the giants in the land. They are the salt of the earth; their threshing floors are full of wheat, and their vats overflow with new wine and oil (see Matt. 5:13; Joel 2:24).

They are children of the Most High, made alive with His DNA for such a time as this.

> *"Man shall not live by bread alone; but man lives by every word that proceeds from the mouth of the Lord"* (Deuteronomy 8:3).

About Dr. Tim Bagwell

Dr. Tim Bagwell has more than 40 years of ministerial experience, more than 30 years as a Senior Pastor, and more than 27 years dedicated to Word of Life Christian Center. He is highly sought after, both nationally and internationally, because of the proven accuracy of his prophetic gift. Many church leaders esteem him as the prophetic voice to their church.

With Dr. Bagwell as the Senior Pastor, Word of Life Christian Center is known as an anointed house of excellence in which the uncompromised Word is preached and signs and wonders follow. Word of Life is located in the greater Denver metropolitan area.

For more information about Dr. Bagwell or Word of Life Christian Center, please visit our website at www.wolcc.net. Other questions, comments, or speaking engagement requests may be submitted via email to pastorbagwell@wolcc.net or by phone at 303-798-5025.

In the right hands, This Book will Change Lives!

Most of the people who need this message will not be looking for this book. To change their lives, you need to put a copy of this book in their hands.

> *But others (seeds) fell into good ground, and brought forth fruit, some a hundred-fold, some sixty-fold, some thirty-fold* (Matthew 13:8).

Our ministry is constantly seeking methods to find the good ground, the people who need this anointed message to change their lives. Will you help us reach these people?

> *Remember this—a farmer who plants only a few seeds will get a small crop. But the one who plants generously will get a generous crop* (2 Corinthians 9:6).

EXTEND THIS MINISTRY BY SOWING

3 BOOKS, 5 BOOKS, 10 BOOKS, **OR MORE TODAY,**

AND BECOME A LIFE CHANGER!

Thank you,

Don Nori Sr., Founder
Destiny Image
Since 1982